Adopted Girls

Hila Haelyon

Adopted Girl
You're a Woman Now
*Body and Identity
Experiences of Women
Adopted in Israel*

π | **Pardes** Publishing

PARDES PUBLISHING
1204 Granger Ave., Ann Arbor, MI 48104, USA

Copyright © 2011 by Pardes Publishing

Translation from Hebrew: Seree Cohen Zohar

First published 2011

Printed in the United States of America

Library of Congress Cataloging in Publication data

Haelyon, Hila.
Adopted Girl: You're a Woman Now / Hila Haelyon
    p.   cm.
Includes bibliographical references and index.
ISBN 978-1-61838-000-5 (hardback)
1. Women.   2. Parenthood.   I. Title
HQ755.7-759.9   2011
301.176.956.94 – dc22
Library of Congress Control Number: 2011932026
ISBN 978-1-61838-000-5 Hardback

Table of Contents

Prologue

A Personal Narrative

Were I to describe my status objectively, I would have to say that I actually have two mothers. One is a good mother, and the other is a good mother. One carried me in her womb, and the other raised and nurtured me. They are unaware of this, but in my perception, they wove a secret pact between them, an unconscious alliance in which one carries in the womb but whose difficult personal circumstances drive her to hand over the child of that womb, and the other standing alongside as helper, her hands open and ready to adapt and adopt. In the *objective* sense of this description, they have in effect created a 'coalition of feminists' in the course of which one mobilizes her self for the sake of the other. In this same *objective* sense, they are even similar. My birth mother took her farewell from me immediately after my birth, and with great suffering: she sent me into the world wrapped in a sheet and a name. The name she bestowed on the day I was born was her request and wish that my life be successful. The name was her vouchsafe, the lingering touch of her motherhood, her connection with my life. My adoptive mother changed my name, embedding a new identity into my being, and just like my birth mother, my adoptive mother also chose a name that was directed only at goodness. In the *objective* sense, I discovered later that the numerical values of both names were identical.

But in the *subjective* sense of the experience, these two mothers exist in my heart and soul, these past thirty-five years, in a continuous, complex dialogue. They appear alongside each other whenever I am faced with making a choice, every time I deliberate, with each decision and all experiences. They are no longer quite as similar, and their dialogue polarizes them. They struggle over forming my present being, over who I was and who I will be, as though tugging at opposite ends of a long rope. One end of that rope is sealed in the wax of the genetic, as red as blood. The other is sealed in a white cape, of culture. So they tug and pull at the rope and over the years, it has thickened and become me.

In the *subjective* sense, my identity is like the moon's appearances: sometimes full and round, clear and whole, unifying the genetic and the cultural, and at other times, I am no more than a crescent. And as with the moon, *what can be seen depends upon the angle of viewing, and the degree of obscurement.* My explanation for this is that in my adopted life, some questions surface repeatedly but will never find satisfying responses. So, from the *subjective* angle, whenever I cannot avail myself of an answer, I may experience a range of emotions: on occasion I am accepting and comforted, and other times, angry and mournful, *and these moods depend on the angle and degree of shadowing.*

The knowledge that I was adopted was never concealed. On the contrary, my parents read "My Story" to me nightly at bedtime, a kind of cultish practice that for Israeli adoptive parents of the 1970s manifested the mantra of the competent authorities of that time. I remember the book's cover well: a soft pink background, flowers spread everywhere, and an illustration of a smiling, blond-crested infant holding a flower stem. On the cover, were the following lines: "*My Story – a story for an adopted girl. Narrated by: Naomi ben-Yisrael. Illustrations: Shmuel Katz*".

Nightly, like the study of doctrine, the rhyming opening lines began as follows: "This is the story of little Yael, and her mother and father. Mommy, Daddy and Yael are a complete family. Daddy's name is Shmuel, and Mommy's name is Naomi. And their little girl is Yael."

My mother received the book from the Department of Child Services; she always spoke with a tone of some awe when referring to them. Just like an obedient soldier, she was careful to conduct herself according to their every guideline, these guidelines only ever conveyed verbally. She was diligent about reading the book to me in the exactly prescribed 'dosages', and even readied herself for the "Dolls and Teddy-bears Hugging Time" exactly as she was taught by the respected Child Services representative. My mother wanted the whole process to be successful. She hoped that I would internalize and understand the special concept of adoption. To this end, she did her utmost to make her/ our family a coherent unit in the most adaptive manner. Together we adopted the white teddy-bear, the dancing doll, the black and white penguin, and in fact, all the toys in my lavish playroom. I adopted them, hugging these or those of them, and she adopted me.

In this way, I always *knew* about my adoption. That knowledge was never a dramatic discovery but rather, all was open and clear. *It was only when I gave birth to my own twin daughters, much later, that I understood the issue of adoption.*

My first pregnancy occurred only after several years of fertility treatments, during which period I worried myself with innumerable questions related to genetics and heredity. These questions remain unanswered. I moved from one treatment to the next like a well-oiled machine, because "I would do everything possible for a child". The macabre and most paradoxical question of all, of why *I* have no children, was resolved successfully through innovative fertility technologies. It was only after the artificial was introduced into my life, that the natural took hold. My skilled physician implemented cutting-edge techniques and I duly succeeded in becoming pregnant with twins. When I arrived at hospital with serious preeclampsia, the doctors battled for my life, and the lives of my fetuses. In the framework of the completely artificial birth by caesarian section, they were extracted into this world. I had become a mother.

This was the significant turning point in my life, particularly that afternoon. It was feeding time in the nursery. I remember it being about 2 p.m. and I was lying on my bed, in pain from the operation. The nurse arrives: her routine includes wheeling the cribs to the mothers' rooms. She enters mine, leaving two cribs near the door. The babies are calm. Inside each crib is a little feeding bottle. The nurse has left me alone with the babies – but they are there far away by the door, and here I am in my bed… and an ocean, a great abyss, all of five meters, gapes between us. With the speed of thought displayed by an animal who must survive, I assess the distance between bed and door. I realize I will need to get down from the bed by myself and quickly roll the cradles across that space. A recurring mantra echoes in my mind: they must not be left alone, I must have them alongside me as quickly as possible. It is too dangerous over there. Here it safe. In retrospect, there was nothing rational about that thought. Taking into consideration my medical condition, I had been assigned a room to myself. No other mother shared my room: no one else could call for help. This actually made the 'private' room an even worse situation for me to overcome.

My babies do not cry. Their breaths are tranquil. It is I who cannot abide the feeling of their being so distanced from me. It is I who needs to handle this 'problem': how to rise and reach them, while in such pain, but gripped by consternation, there was no room for pain. I simply would have to succeed. I toss the pillow aside, grasp the edge of the bed, and throw my legs onto the floor, straightening slowly, and holding onto anything I could find along the way, gritting my teeth with self-conviction: "Mother is here, mother's coming, don't worry". The pain knifes through my flesh: just one more step, one more small movement forward and there! My hand catches hold of both cribs together, I breathe with relief, draw both towards me, collapse back onto the bed. I could barely comprehend what had happened in that instant, why my heart was beating so powerfully. It was as though an eagle had circled above my head, but now had passed and we were safe. I look at my girls. They sleep on. In fact, at this very moment, what can I do for them? I cannot breastfeed. I look at them, my two dolls, wrapped in their newborn peacefulness. My heart fills, my eyes spill their tears – obscuring.

There is a knock at the door, and here she is, beaming. This is the 'close friendship instinct'. Always, throughout my life, she knows when to arrive. My friend, my sister, also adopted. We 'met' at the age of two months. We spent two months of our lives in the infant's houses until her parents and mine met in a group set up by the Child Services for adopting parents. Since then and to date we have stayed together, watching over each other, sensing each other's lives, always there for each other, using the same language, the language of adoption.

She approaches me, hugs me and asks, in her soft voice: "Hilli, what's up?" I am incapable of answering, but I do not need to. She just looks inside those cribs and my twins are reflected back to us, reflected in their silence, which thunders in the room and shakes us both. She, my special and much loved friend, asks the big question, the "how", the question that carries so much significance for us both through the different stages of our lives. Abandonment flutters in the room like a bird with a wounded wing. Sorrow casts a gloomy shadow on all four of us. I think of Hope Edelman: "Sorrow is not linear, nor expected, nor smooth and subdued. Sorrow works in cycles, one ends and another commences." Now I begin to comprehend: emotionally, physically, identifiably, the true meaning of adoption. And it is precisely now that I have such difficulty in understanding: obscuration. Then everyone begins to arrive, and the moon is whole again.

Finally, I return home with my daughters, and begin changing diapers and dressing them, bathing and holding them. My mother and mother-in-law are there to help: they know what to do. I try to learn, and develop my own way of doing. It is only there, in the darkness of night, when my beloved babies are quiet, that I find myself whispering: "How? How, how…?" It is a question that, at least for now, chokes any attempt on my part to try and sing them a lullaby, because the classic songs call on fathers to return from the jobs, and mothers to come to their children. I hum an old tune to myself: "The wind taps at the window, but I'm not afraid at all; come, Mother, come, Mother, sit alongside til I grow up." But you don't have to, really you don't. If you can't come, I will manage. Though what does that say of my daughters? That they will also manage without me?

Eventually I found a disc labeled "Lullabies", but it's an odd set of music, with happy, bouncy melodies. Yes, this is music that suits us just fine. An adopted mother cannot say such things out loud, the things that go through my mind, as such ponderings and delving, questions and considerations, are not considered legitimate, especially when one is not only adopted, but also a past-patient of fertility treatments. The socio-cultural message is: "Be thankful for what you have, and enjoy what there is, and somewhere along the way, if it's not too difficult for you, try to spare a thought or two for your mother who has become a grandmother for the first time in her life".

The question of "How – how does one abandon one's baby?" is not a legitimate one compared to the understanding and empathy expected of me, now a mother myself, towards my biological mother. I have just become a mother, so I realize how difficult it is to care for an infant: how could a young, helpless woman of no means possibly have managed this? It would be far better that I ask no questions. And were I to ask, who could offer an answer?

The experience of desertion, seared as it is in the consciousness of every adopted daughter, causes us to become aware, challenged mothers, our grasp on our children unrelenting as we seek to do it all alone and manage by ourselves. We need no help. The experience of desertion, which shapes the framework of our motherhood, highlights the fragility of the mother-child timeline, and the liquidity of the mother-child presence. In the awareness beating in our lives, the absence of our mother can very suddenly, without any indicator, flicker and flash, leaving us deficient.

These are the silenced experiences I bore for a very long time. I had no one with whom to test my feelings, and even when I did so, I felt I was not always understood. The need to ask others, to share doubts and uncertainties, held its place inside me for a long time. In my life, there is one arena where I am always allowed to ask, where I am encouraged to ask, where I am expected to question and examine. That is the sphere of research, my holy of holies. In research, one must ask. Asking is allowed. Asking anything! And everything! And so it happened that, with the birth of my twin girls in a hospital in central Israel, the birth of a new study surfaced: a study that would research the transition of adopted daughters into biological mothers. The idea was archived and suspended while I focused on another research dealing with women in Israel undergoing fertility treatments.

Six years later, I gave birth to my son, "of black curls, and clever"[1] by natural conception. On the second day of his life I entered the nursery, and after taking care of all his needs and placing him back in his crib, I approached one of the nurses and asked where the babies intended for adoption were located. She was shocked at the question, and wanted to know why I was inquiring. I tried to avoid a full response, which made her angrier. She asked me not to ask such things anymore. I left the nursery shamed and embarrassed, reprimanding myself for my own strange questions. Now I realize that the birth of my son brought the issues of adoption under even closer scrutiny: natural conception and one child are circumstances of similarity with my own birth. The attempt to clarify where infants intended for adoption were held was a feeble effort at trying to patch up another bit of my self-identity.

I returned home with my son, and together we set out on a very different and special journey, two years during

---

1 From the Hebrew poem, *Barren*, 1928, by Israeli national poetess Rachel Bluwstein

which my mother-identity was challenged repeatedly. One of the predominant indicators of difficulty in settling my own sense of motherhood relative to my son appeared in the form of sudden night-time awakenings, during which the baby could not identify me or my spouse, and cried ceaselessly with great noisy gulps. These were episodes lasting some twenty minutes and from which he eventually extracted himself, as though unaware of the intense storm he aroused within himself and within us not two minutes earlier! The explanation I received was that this was a known phenomenon of nightmares, and I was given an array of tests for him. We tried everything: stories at bedtime, relaxing music, midnight walks during which my partner would take the baby in his arms and walk up and down the boulevard for what seemed like hours. Testing continued.

One night, however, all the tests became irrelevant when my son, in the throes of his storm of crying, turned to me and in his baby language, said: "I want my Imma."[2] What horror! I was so badly shaken that I was left speechless, dumbfounded and unable to react. But when this incident repeated itself, I taught myself to hug him close and say: "Imma's here with you". On other occasions, when this statement did not comfort him, I would say: "Let's go together to your Imma". Then I would take his hand and lead him to my bed, tuck him in next to me, stroke his hair and listen to the gasps that followed crying.

My motherhood experience of my son was nothing like my experience with my daughters. They did challenge me emotionally, but the main challenges in their first years of their lives were physical. By comparison, my son challenged me at the deepest emotional and psychological

2 Hebrew for mother.

levels. Mothering him was a rigorous scrutiny that fretted every nerve of my soul, ripping scars open and leaving me bleeding. More especially, I was left with the sense of not knowing.

During those first two years, I tried to assure myself that I needed to learn how to understand *him*; I asked myself how to define *his* difficulties. In the third year, I gave up and focused on trying to explain *my difficulty*. Explanations provided by experts did not help at all. The cure was found in a narrative I concocted for myself. My narrative was that my "black curly-headed one" was teaching me something about my mothering, possibly the most important lesson of my life. I can be a mother. I can be a mother who does not abandon, who stays, who adopts him each time anew, each time when he wakes at night, struck with a fit of crying, seeking 'his Imma'.

It was during this period that my need to discuss the experience of mothering with other adopted women began to consolidate. I wanted to learn about their experiences, hoping that along the way, some light would be shed on mine too. As with every qualitative research, the birth of an idea is also accompanied by the death of parts of that idea. My journey of clarification had just begun but it was those interviewees who, sharing their narratives with me, taught me to think about the reality of an adopted daughter's life in a more complex and different way. Their narratives caused a turn in my thoughts, and the scope of the research broadened and moved forward.

Through many hours of interviews and conversations, these women taught me that not only the transition to motherhood is reflective but that these reflections exist throughout every cycle of the adopted woman's life. Reflections appear whenever the adopted woman understands she is different or unique compared to her friends, other relatives, and to her parents. Reflections surface at adolescence, in overseas student exchange programs, when choosing which professional field to study, and even in the food one teaches oneself to eat, immediately on opening the adoption file.

Initially, I persist in remaining close to the research framework I have established: a discourse on the adopted woman's transition to biological motherhood. Later, I capitulate, the research agenda dissipates, the boundaries are breached, and the research which seeks to hear the voices of these women and unify their experiences, takes on a life of its own. Like me, they feel that the discourse isolates the place of adoptive parents and biological parents. When speaking on their own behalf, they were expert in using quantitative tools to examine the adaptation of "adopted girls", the scope of anxiousness, and the nature of communication employed by "adopted girls", and more. In quantitative studies, they were always related to with the measuring tools applied by experts, and these were the terms in which they learned to think of themselves. In quantitative studies they were documented with a somewhat patronizing perspective, and remained "adopted little girls". With every interview I conducted, with every question I chose to ask, another complex world was revealed, a unique and sometimes hair-raising narrative.

Slowly I begin to comprehend the complexities and the ethical obligations I have towards "biological birthers", a term that the interviewees insist I use when referring to the biological mother. The interviewees' narratives become mirrors in which I shatter into a thousand slivers and then gel again. I want to explore their views on their biological mothers, but they have a more urgent agenda, one that encompasses questions of identity and body, descriptions comprised of early childhood and puberty, stories of opening adoption files and their relationship with their biological mothers.

This study is difficult, almost too difficult for me to bear: I want to set limits, and they want to break them and the dams and the silences. I capsize, eventually. Capitulating to that unique value known as "researcher's flexibility", I am swept with these women into hours upon hours of interviews, descriptions, narratives, superlatives, metaphors and similes. Fatigue and frustration are my escorts as I feel my way blindly through the unknown, until a moment of clarity surfaces: their stories, my story, the combined stories of us all, are narratives that describe the continuum of our lives. Adoption is not an experience that can be fenced into a specific instant, a particular hour, a perfunctory look. Adoption begins with the moment of birth, but who knows when it ends? As one interviewee said: *We, how shall I say, as soon as we are born, we're tossed into the world … and they forget to catch us.*

Introduction

Adoption in Israel

> Once upon a time, many years ago, there was a hen who could not
> lay eggs. The poor hen very much wanted an egg of her own. She
> waited and waited, until one day, from out of nowhere, an egg
> rolled across, next to her. She sat and brooded over it for many
> hours... sitting, brooding until at last, a cute little chick hatched
> ... this is how, in kindergarten, I was told that I'm adopted.
> (Description by an interviewee participating in the study).

There are two main forms of adoption in Israel: internal
adoptions, and international adoptions. Internal adoptions
are of children born in Israel to Israeli mothers. International
adoption is conducted through associations established for
this purpose, which began operations in Israel in 1998.
Israeli law obligates social workers appointed by the
State to accompany the process in accordance with "the
understandings of the Hague Convention" (Perlmutter &
Birman, 2005). However, international adoptions in Israel
already commenced informally around the end of the
1980s. It was a private event, conducted through agents,
with infants primarily being brought from South America,
and later also from Romania (Noy-Sharab, 2004). The
legalized arrangement was passed in 1996, although the
relevant associations only began operations in 1998.

The current study focuses specifically on adoptions
of the first kind, within Israel, of children born in Israel

and adopted by Israeli families. This book presents the narratives of fifteen adopted women, most of whom became biological mothers. The narratives move between different time frames in their lives: early childhood, adolescence, opening the adoption file, meeting the biological mother, and finally, transitioning into motherhood and parenthood.

Much has been written on international adoption, on the experiences of being an adopting parent, and experiences of the biological mothers (chiefly from overseas) have been recorded, but it seems that the experience of the adopted daughter is still very much a marginal aspect. With this book, I seek to expose the copability of Israeli women who themselves are adopted daughters by exploring the prism of the family life cycle, and emphasizing the feminine experience of being adopted.

Israel – Inland Adoption

Exodus, Chapter 2 (verses 2-10 inclusive), presents the first testimony of the existence of adoption in Jewish life:

> 2: And the woman conceived, and gave birth to a son, and saw that he was a delight, and she concealed him for three moons; 3: and when she could no longer conceal him, she took an ark of bulrushes, coating it with slime and pitch, and placed the child within, and placed it on the brink of the Nile river. 4: And his sister stood off a way, to know what would be done with him. 5: And Pharaoh's daughter came down to the river to bathe, and her maidens walked along the river's edge; and she saw the ark among the bulrushes and sent her maid to bring it. 6: And she opened it and saw him, the child; the boy wept, and she felt compassionate towards him, saying: "This is one of the

Hebrew's children". 7: Then his sister said to Pharaoh's daughter: "Shall I go and call for a woman from among the Hebrews, to nurse the child for you?". 8: And Pharaoh's daughter said to her: "Go", and the girl went and called *the child's mother*. 9: And Pharaoh's daughter said to her: "Take this child away, and nurse it for me, and I will give you your wages". And *the woman took the child* and nursed him. 10: And the child grew, and she brought him to Pharaoh's daughter, and *he was a son for her*. And she called his name Moses, saying: "It is because I drew him from the water".

A careful study of these Biblical verses discloses the complex triangulated relationship of biological mother—child—adoptive mother. The dialogue taking shape in the space between biological mother and adoptive mother is characterized by scrutinized choices of words to describe the figures of the women. First, the description of separation from the biological child is conducted within the emotional complexity involving surrender of the child: it is only after three months of attempts at concealment, efforts to keep the biological offspring in the family, that the decision is made to remove him from the home. No easy decision, this, as seen by the Biblical narrator's word choices: *when she could no longer* describes the status of the mother compelled to hand over her son. The act of transfer is no easy matter either, and is accompanied by words clearly indicating protectiveness and anxiety over the son's fate.

This little bundle of a human being is concealed like treasure in an ark, and the biological mother sends the infant's sister to watch how things eventuate. The new relationship formed with the adoptive mother occurs through the agency of the biological mother, and only after the infant is drawn out of the water does the sister approach, and cleverly suggest the services of a wet nurse. As soon as Pharaoh's daughter agrees to the arrangement, the infant's sister calls *the child's mother*. We note that at this point the biological mother is still called *mother*.

Now we must take note of an interesting development. The Biblical narrator chooses a new terminology, which would indicate her status as being separated from Moses: immediately on having weaned the child, the mother is called *the woman*. Throughout this text, Moses himself is variously called *the child* or *the boy*, indicating a status of not fully belonging to either woman. Only after being brought to Pharaoh's daughter, to be raised by her, is he referred to with the term *a son*. The phrasing *he was a son for her* alludes to the fact that only through the institution of adoption, and with the foundation of the parent-child relationship, is Moses given an identity that connects him with a family: a new family headed by Pharaoh's daughter, who is both an adoptive mother and single mother.

Nonetheless, the word choices clearly describe Moses' status as *the son of* rather than the Egyptian princess as *the mother of*. The Biblical narrator is pedantic in describing the simultaneous complexity of the mothering relationship for both the biological and the adoptive mothers, and in this way ensures that the position of the biological mother remains respected.

This brief excerpt provides a fascinating perspective into how the framework of adoption exposes the raw nerves and sensitive convolutions accompanying the interaction between the parties involved. Further scrutiny indicates that the status of the biological father is silenced. Thus it seems that the Israeli legislature, well aware of this complexity, encompassed it in its Child Adoption Law [5741–1981], which qualifies the government institution known as "The Child Services" as the only body authorized to operate on all adoption-related issues in Israel. The Child Services acts as part of the Ministry of Welfare's Department for Social and Personal Services (Levy-Schiff, 2001).

The background document presented in January 2002 to the Committee for Labor, Welfare and Health describes the Service's activities, objectives, and the professional status of its employees. The very choice of the organization's name, *Child Services* [Hebrew – literal: 'services for the sake of the child'], indicates the ideological concept behind the organization's activities as a body whose purpose is to promote the welfare of adopted children. However, Child Services also covers additional populations such as pregnant teens, unwed pregnancy, families waiting to adopt, and adult adoptees interested in opening their adoption files. As part of its inland adoption activities, the Child Services mediates three factors: the biological mother interested in registering her newborn for adoption, the child who is the adoptive candidate, and the family interested in adopting within the framework of psycho-social parenting.

Research studies conducted worldwide indicate the dramatic reduction in percentages of inland adoptions compared to international adoptions. The researchers claim that processes of globalization and the ensuing thriving of mediating organizations and parties have expanded adoption possibilities (Brodzinsky & Palacios, 2005). This fact, taken together with the complexity and discretion required in closed adoption, also projects onto the approach taken by the State of Israel. Further studies conducted in recent years indicate that despite the institution of adoption drawing on the humanitarian view that every child is entitled to be raised in a fixed, parental home (although the parents chose to surrender the child), there are still situations defined as "disruptive adoptions" (Fisher, 2003; Schwartz, 2006). Disruptive adoptions are defined by the researcher Lita Linzer Schwartz (2006) as adoptions that began routinely but during the course of proceedings, the adopting parents decided not to follow the process through to the end. She explains the reasons behind why adoptions fail, and claims that the psychological and legal intricacies of adoption contain many factors that may lead to cessation of the process. These include, for example, the biological mother refusing to uphold her agreement to transfer the child and canceling the arrangement; the intervention of the biological father who may refuse to let the process continue; the unsuitability of the child to the adoptive parents; and the adoptive parent's inability to adapt.[1] Linzer Schwartz explained that such situations may cause numerous emotional and psychological problems in the child, damage to the child's self-confidence, reinforcement of the sense of rejection, feelings of guilt and shame, and in the child's future, even the sense of inability to establish trusting relationships. In extreme cases, the second rejection is experienced by the child as a very real trauma (Schwartz, 2006).

1 In work done by Festinger (2002), this phenomenon was reported as commencing during the 1980s relevant to 10-25 percent of all adoptions. With regard to young children, the rate of failure stands at 9-10 percent, but with older children the failure rate is some 25 percent. By contrast, Barth and Berry (1998) claimed that the failure rates are: less than 1% for infants; 10% for children aged 6 to 12 years old; and 13% for children aged 12 to 18 years. Researchers are also divided on the issue of increased rate of failure over the years. Festinger claimed that since 1988, the rate of adoption failure has remained fixed. Both studies indicate increased possibilities of successful adoption as the socio-economic status increases, but no differences were found for the nature of the family unit, whether comprised of heterosexual or same-sex couples relative to the rates of success or failure.

Inland adoptions in Israel are offered via several routes. *The first route* is geared to childless couples seeking to adopt their first child. In the framework of this route, up to two children can be adopted. A child wohse the biological parents signed a waiver of parental rights is defined as *infant* until the age of two years old. The potentially adoptive parents join the adoption list, although they can simultaneously continue to receive fertility treatment towards realizing biological parenthood. The wait time with this adoption method averages some five years. The couple must be married, and the marriage must be recognized by the Ministry of the Interior. Their ability to financially provide for a child must also be proven. Additionally, legislation determines that for the first route, the age difference between the adoptive parents and the infant shall be no more than 43 years. If, during the adoption waiting period, the couple has managed to realize biological parenthood, whether through fertility treatments or natural conception, they can choose to remain on the adoption list or opt out and allow their place to be taken by the next couple in line.

The second route is to receive an infant via queue jumping. This would occur when the infant to be adopted is found to have a medical or developmental problem, a genetic complexity, or an infant showing drug addiction and needing rehabilitation. Other situations include infants who may have a non-normative appearance, or children with whom the biological parents insist on maintaining a relationship, the latter known as 'open adoption'. If a couple expresses interest in receiving a special needs infant, the waiting period can shorten to two years or less. Welfare representatives maintain the 43-year maximum age difference for this adoption route, too.

The third route relates to adoption of older children, aged two to 11 years. Children are divided by age groups: (1) pre-schoolers; and (2) school age. Child Services tries, in this adoption route, to maintain sibling relationships and transfer siblings together for adoption.[2]

All the adoption routes described above contain several formal phases of interaction between the adoptive families and the Child Services representatives. The initial stage involves the interested couple contacting one of the Child Services centers. The couple is then provided with registration forms and explanatory material. Once the forms are completed and returned, an appointment is set for a frontal meeting between the couple and the Child Services representative. If the couple is childless, a psychological evaluation is conducted through the privately operated Pilat Institute, a psychometric testing center in Israel, independent of the Child Services. If the couple already has children, the evaluation is carried out by a Child Services social worker.[3]

In addition to the psychological assessment, the couple must prove medical competence. The Child Services representatives are responsible for conducting a search in police files to clarify the couple's past ("Certificate of Integrity"). All forms dealing with "parental capability" are presented to the authorizing committee. In all the adoption

2 From a statement by Ella Blas, May 2002, in the "Reshet" television channel's program "Open House".
3 This issue often arouses resistance in adoptive parents who claim that biological parents are not required to undergo evaluation before bringing children into the world and therefore it is unfair for the adoptive parents to be required to invest monetary and emotional resources at the outset of the adoption process. These evaluations cause noticeable anxiety to potential adopters the evening prior to the evaluation appointment (data from Child Services).

frameworks, the prospective adoptive parents join a "preparatory group" appropriate to the adoption route they have chosen.

When the waiting period reaches its official termination, the couple is sent an invitation to receive the child. From the day of adoption and throughout the following six months, the Child Services follows up on the child's assimilation into the adopting family. During this period, the child is still officially under Child Services guardianship. Follow-up includes visits by a Child Services representative to the adoptive couple's home. If Child Services reports are positive, the couple then applies to court to legalize the adoption through an "Adoption Order". Child Services simultaneously sends its approval to court and the official adoption order is produced. The child is added to the parents' documentation and becomes their legal child. A new identity card is prepared for the child, whose name is then removed from the ID cards of the biological parents. In this way, the child disconnects from the biological parents and legally connects to the adoptive parents, leaving no way for the biological parents to trace him or her.[4]

In Israel, as with other countries, two approaches are employed relative to adoptions: one is known as *closed adoption*, and the other is *open adoption*. Closed adoption means that the adopted child and the biological parents are unable to contact each other. There is no continuum to the

---

4 Families and couples, as well as single mothers and fathers, who wish to realize their adoptive rights relative to an older child, undergo a multi-phase process culminating in the National Committee for Special Needs Children, where matches are made between the child and the parental ability to help that child. The adoptive parent receives full information concerning the child

relationship between biological parents and the child.[5]

Open adoption is a framework that allows preserving the connection between the adoptive parents, the adopted child and the biological parents. The connection may take the form of meetings, exchange of correspondence, video clips or exchange of information via the welfare officer. The decision to authorize open adoption can only be taken by the Family Court, which meticulously examines the biological family's ability to respect the boundaries of adoption and acknowledge the rights of the adoptive parents to be real parents for the adoptee. Within the framework of decisions concerning open adoption, broad scope is made for the nature of the adoptive family and their emotional threshold in coping with the experience. However, the Child Services clarifies that "the child's best interests" are its primary priority, far and beyond any court decision. Due to the complex nature of open adoption, the Child Services escorts the adopting family by providing individual and group therapy (via the Child Services organization).

Researchers comparing open and closed adoption claim that the global trend, appearing in the USA and Canada, and in European countries, is moving towards open adoption. They further claim that the emotional and psychological consequences of open adoption need to be explored relative to the adopted children, the biological parents and the adoptive parents. Supporters of open adoption claim that the dispensation of secrecy from the adoption process is not only moral but positively projects on all parties involved in structuring the familial relationship. These researchers

---

5   By law, contact can only be renewed when the adoptee reaches the age of 18 years, should the adoptee wish to open the adoption file to seek the source family.

claim that the greater the openness between the members of the new family, the more the feelings of uncertainty and insecurity are reduced between the adoptive and biological parents. This open arrangement would also undermine the uncertainty, anxiety and fear of the biological mother as to the fate of the child she gave up for adoption. At the same time, open adoption extends the sense of the biological mother's control over procedures that often are enforced on her. Furthermore, say the supporters of this method, open adoption is a more appropriate alternative for the adopted child her- or himself, as it lessens the sense of rejection and loss of the biological parents and this immediately projects, in turn, on reinforcing the child's self-confidence, heightening self-image, and reducing possible adaptation difficulties (Brodzinsky, 2005; Sykes, 2001).

By contrast, those opposing open adoption claim that it is the very fact of connection with the biological source family that can lead the child into feeling lack of control and confidence in her or his relationship with the adoptive parents. Such an experience would be disruptive to the desired communication between the adopted child and the new family, and undermine the adoptive parents' sense of entitlement in their relationship with the child. Opponents of open adoption claim that the adopted child will be caused confusion, poor self-confidence, and inability to communicate with her or his new family (Brodzinsky, 2005; Cocozzelli, 1989).

As part of the *Child Adoption Law 1981*, legislature determined that from the age of 18 years and up, adoptees are entitled to open their adoption files and receive details of their biological family. Child Services maintains all details concerning the circumstances of adoption and the biological parents for every adoptee in Israel. The Child

Adoption Law allows only the adoptees themselves to open the adoption file: the biological parent is not entitled to this right. The request is carried out in several phases. The first stage requires a written request to the Child Services national center in Jerusalem. The adoptee details her or his name, age, and all other required personal details needed. A Child Services representative will then contact the adoptee seeking to open the adoption file to arrange a meeting, with follow-up meetings intended to become better acquainted with the adoptee and prepare the adoptee for coping with the information that will be conveyed.

If the adoptee remains interested in contacting the biological mother, the Child Services acts as mediating party, by contacting the Child Services representing the biological mother. The encounter between adoptee and biological mother only becomes possible if the mother agrees to it. Such encounters generally take place in the Child Services offices with a social worker present.[6]

On occasion, however, the adoptee's request may be met by refusal by the biological family. This leaves the adoptee in a state of helplessness, as such a refusal seals the fate of adoptees' attempts at realizing the sense of structuring a whole identity. In this context, Israeli researchers raise interesting questions related to the ethics and legalities of the adoptees' rights to trace their biological parents. Ruth Zafran claims that the essence of the paradox is

6 Israel is deficient in methodical research of the number of requests to open adoption files, compared to non-request numbers. There is also no methodical research relative to the number of mothers refusing to meet their biological child compared to those who agree to such contact. Furthermore, there is lack of methodical qualitative research on the nature of the meeting with the biological mother, and the experience of opening an adoption file.

characterized by the reversed tendency apparent in the various motivations of adoptee and biological parent. While the biological parent refuses to create a situation of encounter and seeks to minimize exposure of details, the adoptees seek to broaden their scope of information and learn about their biological biography. In her view, this disparity leads to a state where the adoptees are denied their basic right to trace their identity. Zafran adds that the Child Adoption Law [5741] 1981, legislated as a result of the Etzioni Committee Report, further reduced the adoptee's rights in this regard. Section 30, still currently valid, determined issues relating to the adoption file such that the file will not be accessible for viewing except in the presence of the government's legal advisor, the registrar of marriages (for that purpose only), and the chief welfare office. This situation will exist only:

> By request of an adoptee who has reached 18 years old [...] the welfare officer is entitled to allow the adoptee to peruse the relevant registered file. Should the welfare officer refuse the request, the court is entitled to allow perusal after receiving the welfare officer's review.

According to Zafran, this determination allows at least partial recognition of the right to trace biography, in that it allows the adoptee to peruse the adoption file which includes, as noted, identifying information on the adoptee's biological parents or, at the very least, the biological mother. The right in principle of adult adoptees to be exposed to the registered information is admittedly subject to the welfare officer's considerations, but does not negate the existence of the right in principle.

Should the welfare officer refuse to allow perusal, the

adoptee can apply to court to request assistance. According to Zafran, a paradox exists between the textuary meaning of the instruction relative to the accepted approach in the framework of internal instructions prepared by Child Services: on one hand, the right to perusal exists in principle although implementation is dependent on the welfare officer's consideration, while on the other hand the internal instructions of the Child Services employs a rigorous procedure with regard to conveying data in the adoption file. The Child Services internal procedures requires meeting adoptees and preparing them for opening the file, and information is only conveyed in the second meeting. However, at this stage, identifying information on the biological parents is not conveyed although general details are provided, such as descriptions of the mother, her status and education, her origin and the circumstances leading to adoption. The scope and nature of this information varies from one file to another. In most cases, it is very limited.

All this may lead to independent attempts to trace the biological parents, a difficult and exhausting journey in search of wholeness of identity. Zafran states that even if groups and forums are created for the purpose of providing outlets and support, the harsh experience of blankness relative to identity nonetheless remains. As a result, Zafran sums up her work with the claim that in a substantial number of Western legal methods, and especially the USA, Australia and Western Europe, significant legal changes have been implemented. The overall policy guiding methods up until two decades ago was strictly one of immunity and negation of the right to information of any form whatsoever. Since the beginning of the 1990s, approaches increasingly adopted methods that acknowledge the right to trace sources, if in differing degrees and scope from one method to the next.

Millie Mass, like Zafran, also researches the moral legislative complexities at the core of Israeli adoption policy. Her work focuses on the marginalizing of the perception of loss in the framework of discourse on closed adoption. Mass cites the renowned "Infant of Contention" (2005) case, in which the birth mother handed her infant over for adoption without the biological father's knowledge. Some time later, she reneged and even told the father that he had a son. The couple commenced a dramatic struggle to have the infant returned. The court verdict determined that the infant would remain with the biological parents.

This legal decision emphasizes, in Mass' view, the predominant approach in Israel in which the issue of loss is insufficiently explored relative to closed adoption. In Mass' view, closed adoption is the default in Israel. This method of adoption allows no connection between the adoptee and the biological parents until the child reaches the age of 18 years. Mass feels that the very nature of closed adoption inherently encompasses an experience that ranges from damage to loss for both the child given to adoption and the biological birth mother. In Mass' view:

> The definition of deprivation caused to children not raised by their birth parents ranges from damage to loss. The perception of damage presumes that adoption constitutes compensation for the disappearance of the birth parents from the child's life. The perception of loss presumes that it is impossible to compensate the child for the birth parents' disappearance and that the child's referential relationship cannot be exchanged (Mass, 2008, pg. 6).

The loss of the referential relationship can be perceived as a constant presence and may develop into an identity disorder that creates the sense of loss of self. As a result, claims Mass, it is precisely in a reality in which the process of adoption is defined as a necessary option that it would be preferable to maintain some affinity between the biological birth mother and the child (except in cases where such a relationship would constitute risk to the child's welfare). In this regard, Mass raised a further problem: in her view, because the legal discourse around adoption deals with the child's future, it is inherently related to uncertainty. Furthermore, in order to acknowledge the loss caused to adopted children, it is necessary to acquire their testimony of such, but such testimony is not always accessible, and the aspect of loss then becomes a peripheral discussion. Lastly, claims Mass, Israel has not set a minimal time frame in which the decision to transfer a child for adoption must be made. In her view, women suffering post-partum depression may not be in a mental state appropriate to reaching a realistic decision; similarly, some fathers experience emotional upheavals.[7] Mass further claims that the difficulties encountered by the discourse on loss are a result of the institutionalized structure that qualified Child Services as a body meant to provide solutions for both parties but which finds itself representing conflictual interests. The Child Services is open to pressures from two directions, the biological parents, and the adopting parents. Mass claims that:

---

7   Mass claims that an intermediary report was recently presented to the Ministers of Justice and of Welfare by a committee recommending that parents' requests to transfer a child for adoption be given consideration only two weeks after birth of the child, and subject to evaluating the parent's emotional status.

The adoption officer in contact with both parties is open to pressure by the prospective adoptive candidates as a result of empathy towards the candidates' desire to raise children and the demand, which exceeds supply, for children to adopt. This may be further exacerbated by the socio-economic disparity often present between the birth parents and the prospective adoptive parents who are at a clear advantage (Mass, 2008, pg. 10).

These, and other aspects, lead Mass to state that there is great importance in restoring the subjects of loss and damage to the legal, social, public and ethical discourses relevant to issues of adoption.

Such academic discourses repeatedly emphasize the multiple divergences and ramifications of adoption, which is much like a polyphonic work in a lively range of voices of exposure and sensitivity, weaving and unraveling interconnections between adoptive parents, adopted children, birth parents, and welfare authorities. Nonetheless, the current study offers a unique platform for the narratives and voices of 15 Israeli women, all adopted, who relate to these issues only from their own personal perspectives.

Adoption and the Cycle of Family Life

Sharon Deacon commenced her discussion of questions relating to a definition of the family unit as follows:

What constitutes family? Do genes and blood ties define who belongs in the family? Should family members have a similar appearance? Does the same living space need to be shared, constituting a boundary by which family is defined? Do family members need to be together in order to be considered family? Or perhaps, family is a collection, an organized group of people who share their lives together and provide each other with physical and mental support? Answering these questions is currently far more problematic than it was 100 years ago. Technology, modern civilization, and the development of complex legislative systems have all expanded the definition of what a family actually is (Deacon, 1997, pg. 245).

After exploring the complexity in defining the family unit, Sharon Deacon stated that accessibility of new fertility technologies, same sex marriages, alternative marriages, remarriage, foster families and adoptive family have all enabled the formation of a family unit that does not require the traditional presence of man and woman as life partners in bringing children to the world and raising them. Deacon, having presented these claims, then focused on understanding the cycle of family life through the prism of adoption.

In her view, the starting point of the adoptive family is drawn from the reality of infertility and loss. Most of the couples considering adoption in the USA are couples defined as infertile. The problem of fertility or rather, its absence, causes many to feel a sense of loss and mourning over the biological child they will never succeed in bringing into the world. It is a state of mourning over the loss of biological continuity. Couples diagnosed as infertile perceive infertility as enforced on them, and may often view this status as a kind of punishment from heaven. Being beyond their range of control, it arouses negative emotions. Women unable to become pregnant often feel that they have failed in the mission that should be supremely natural for women; they may lose their sense of femininity and sexuality, and sometimes even feel they have not successfully matured. Men may perceive their masculinity as damaged, or feel unworthy of their female partners.

In the most problematic of cases, a connection is made between fertility and parenthood, where infertile couples 'conclude' that their status as a couple alludes to an incapability of being good parents. Such couples will experience difficulty in expanding the family unit and will forego parenthood. By contrast, couples who succeed in separating problems of infertility from parenting capability will admittedly pass through a period of mourning, but will simultaneously take active steps towards expanding the family unit.

Deacon's (1997) opinion is that the loss of representation through infertility also involves the expanded family: grandparents will experience mourning and frustration over the fact that their genetic legacy will cease to exist. Only after the family members accept the issue of infertility and its accompanying sorrow can they begin to seriously consider adoption. Here, too, the involvement of the expanded family is important, to ensure that the adopted child will not be rejected, especially when the adoptee is via international adoption. It is vital that the couple openly and honestly discuss their feelings about race and racism when considering international adoption. They must give thought to how they will provide suitable tools for their child's coping with fundamental identity issues such as "Who am I?", and how they will teach their child to deal with racism in society. Furthermore, adoptive families must create a social life that maximizes awareness and social acceptance of the other. Once the decision is reached, the family must also take into account that it will be interracial for many generations. Finally, the couple must also be fully aware that such a child will be a constant reminder of the fact that they were unable to conceive and give birth by natural means. Once all these issues are resolved, and the couple nonetheless seeks to adopt, the child will be integrated into the new family framework and the family is then considered 'expanded'.

It must be remembered, however, that in contrast to the process of natural pregnancy, where the couple has nine months in which to acclimate to the idea of new life in the form of a growing, moving fetus, parenthood through adoption is sudden. Transition from the state of childlessness to parenthood can be swift, from one day to the next, for adopting couples. The speed of transition often creates adaptational problems for the adopted child. At the very instant that the infant is placed into the waiting arms of the adopting parents, this first embrace may also arouse various sensations, among them the feeling that the couple is now responsible, for the rest of their lives, for the life of someone else's child. In this regard, Deacon quoted Rosenberg's view that on receiving the child, the adoptive parents also receive the 'ghosts' of the child's biological parents (Rosenberg, 1992 as cited in Deacon, 1997). Sharon Deacon's recommendation is to keep the name that the biological parents gave the child, and add a new name given by the adoptive parents. In this way, at least some minimal amount of the child's earliest biological history remains with her or him as the child integrates in the current, new family unit.

Deacon (1997) described the first year of the child's life as the honeymoon period. In her opinion, this is the critical year for establishing trust between the adopted infant and the adopting parents. This is like the test run period: the infant senses that her or his natural environment has been altered, and may experience that loss of previous environment and develop fear towards the new, adoptive parents. The parents, on the other hand, may experience anger and frustration from their attempts to establish parenthood. Only when the infant has overcome the trauma of separation from the previous environment can the relationship with new parents be established. At this stage, the sense of belonging is felt in the manner in which the infant will now resist strangers. Many adoptive parents have a keen desire to preserve this period, and even perpetuate it. For them, this is the first indicator that their parenting is successful. Nonetheless, in a study of 15 Caucasian couples who adopted 21 Korean children between them, it was reported that from their second year since adoption and on, even children who had acclimated well started showing signs of sleep problems, greater frequency of night crying, anger attacks, hyperactive behaviors, hallucinations, speech impediments, disruptions to focused behaviors over the long term, and obstinate possessiveness of toys and other objects (Kim & Kim, 1979, as cited in Deacon, 1997, pgs. 250-251). Seeking to explain these phenomena, the researchers claimed that the sudden change in environment apparently led to adaptation difficulties and inhibited development in the adopted children. The absence of a fixed care-giver at the outset of the infant's life also created difficulty in internalizing the permanence of, and separating from, the object. Possibly the experience of pre-adoption neglect led to impaired abilities of concentration, discomfort and unwillingness to share and cooperate in these infants. The transition from one set of sleeping habits to another apparently created the sense of fear and abandonment, as prior to adoption these infants had slept well in a room with other infants: only after adoption and being given a room of their own did they translate this isolation into a second rejection. The researchers further pointed to the phenomenon of the Korean children's refusal to connect to and communicate with faces having Asian features. They claimed that these facial features must have flooded the infants with harsh pre-adoption memories. The researchers further claimed that the frequent outbursts of anger and crying at night are manifestations of the infants testing the scope of commitment to them in their adoptive parents, this stage intended to examine the degree of stability and security in their new lives. However, other researchers internationally noted that during their first year of life in the adoptive family, most such infants make significant progress, especially when adopted at a very young age (Tizard, 1991).

When the infant reaches about three years old, and after a relationship of trust is established with the parents, the stage of individuation/separation from the adoptive parents commences. The tangible manifestation is behavioral, 'acting out'; its purpose is to make waves. Adoptive parents may think that this is the expression of some unknown genetic trait in the child. Researchers claim that this behavior is an additional test run in the process of accepting the adoptive parents. On entering an educational framework, the parents must cope with another new reality, during the course of which the child will need to cope with the knowledge of adoption, and may further include coping with a different external appearance if the child adoption was inter- rather than intra-national.

In Sharon Deacon's view, the time frame between 3 to 7 years old constitutes the best time for parents to hold an open, easy-going discussion with their child on the issue of adoption. Parents must prepare their child for coping outside of the family framework with questions and concerns relative to being adopted. This stage is also typified by the child's own interest in exploring and clarifying why she or he was given up for adoption, and who the biological parents were. During this stage, adopted children begin to comprehend that in actuality, they have two sets of parents, biological and adoptive. This may give rise to fantasies and daydreams about the biological parents.

Only at about 6 years old, adopted children reach new understandings of the physical, racial and ethnic differences between themselves and their adoptive parents. Such differences no longer make it possible to maintain secrecy relative to the adoption. Deacon feels it is best for adoptive parents not to deny the physical dissimilarities between them and their children, as denials of this kind merely exacerbate the experience of otherness in the child. Deacon added that at this stage, when the children have relationships with other family members, such as siblings, cousins and so on, adopted children may feel envy or anger towards their extended family, especially in light of these other family members having genetic and biological connections with the family, which further highlight the adopted child's otherness. The related family members, however, might experience the sense of guilt over belonging.

In a therapeutic model geared at coping with such situations, researchers claim that it is the responsibility of the adoptive parents to teach their children how to develop positive perceptions relative to their biological origins. The parents must expose their children to information on their traditional ancestry, and connect them emotionally and positively to their racial group. The next, and most significant, stage that Deacon examined is adolescence, which she terms the maturation years. In her view, research indicates that applications for psycho-clinical treatment reaches its peak among adopted children at around 15 years old, after which less psychological consultation is sought. She stated that "adolescence is a tumultuous time for any family, however being an adoptive family has added stressors" (Deacon, 1997, pg. 252). Adolescent children seek to demonstrate separateness and independence, while simultaneously still being dependent on their parents. This stage may once again manifest among many adopted teens, insecurity being accompanied by fears of rejection and abandonment. According to Deacon, the teen may then feel the desire to leave the family before the family abandons her or him. Adopted teens, more than others, rediscover the lack of similarity between them and their parents, and once again face the concept that closed adoption has caused them to forego, to some degree, part of their identity and self. Seeking identity brings questions to the surface that relate to genetic identity, blood relatives, and the sense of belonging to the primary biological family. Such questions may give rise to a feeling which Deacon termed "genealogical bewilderment". This is a complex phase for the adoptive parents, too, in that they may feel such questions and searching manifest or allude to the child's imminent desertion; the parents may fear loss of their child's love. Such a fear can in turn have the effect of making them sensitive and overly tense when exercising parental authority. Furthermore, Deacon claimed that adolescence in adopted teens whose ethnic identity is different from that of their adoptive parents (where the difference is noticeable due to the absence of physical similarity) will arouse further coping experiences, especially in efforts at balancing the tension between the natural and the cultural: on one hand, such adopted teens have learned to live within the cultural codes of the adoptive families, but on the other hand, their own appearance, being different, makes the teens wonder whether the broader socio-cultural framework would have accepted them more successfully as equals. Deacon claimed that only open avenues of communication between adoptive parents and adopted children, and a supportive social environment, will help the families succeed in managing this stage, and ensure a stable, confident identity for the adopted child.

In research conducted by Hajal and Rosenberg (1991), another aspect of coping in adopted children was emphasized. They felt that because adolescence also involves sexual development and change, adoptive parents must structure clear boundaries between permitted and prohibited when relating to sexuality within the family. This is of even greater importance when the family comprises adopted and biological siblings. Among adopted siblings, an additional fear lurks: that of forming an intimate relationship with a blood relation without conscious intent. This is a central issue in closed adoption, as at this stage the adoptee does not yet know the identity of her or his biological family (Hajal & Rosenberg, 1991). Another matter of concern to the adoptive parents at this stage is that their adopted child should not make the mistake of giving birth to a child for the sake of keeping it, as a compensatory action for the biological mother's "error". In essence, this would often constitute a repetition of the biological mother's mistake of having a child that cannot be suitably cared for by the young birth mother, although the perspective regarding the birth is to keep, rather than abandon, the baby.

The next stage described by Deacon is that of "emptying the nest", of leaving the family home and starting out independently beyond the parental home. Deacon claimed that this is the most difficult stage for adoptive parents and that often, throughout the course of raising the adopted child, the parents feel they are living on borrowed time which progresses from one 'until' to the next: until the child opens the adoption file, until the biological mother is met, and so on. As a result, adoptive parents tend not to encourage the adopted child to 'leave the nest' until the adopted child becomes sufficiently independent and the parents are left little choice in the matter. This stage presages that of finding a partner. According to Deacon, research indicates that adopted children usually prefer to marry a partner of a different race. This helps them overcome the fear that they might unintentionally marry their own sibling or blood relative. During this stage, with the adopted children planning their own future family, questions of genetics, race, and blood ties resurface. The tendency to preoccupation with these issues derives from the adoptees' wish to provide their own offspring with a stable biological genealogy.

Research on the cycle of family life offers little knowledge on how adoptees cope and on their relationships with their adoptive families, claimed Sharon Deacon. Even less information exists on the relationships between adoptees and their own biological children. The only studies conducted have explored moral issues relating to the degree of responsibility that adoptees feel towards their aging adoptive parents: which, as it turns out, appears to be identical to that of biological children to their own parents. In some cases, adoptees have even chosen to open their adoption files only after the adoptive parents have passed away, to avoid hurting the adoptive parents' feelings.

A Mother's Desertion / A Mother's Love

This study seeks to explore the experiences of adopted women, born in Israel and adopted in the framework of closed inland adoptions. The initial research premise was that despite the fact that closed adoption inherently contains broad global and emotional dilemmas which are not necessarily gender specific, the experiences of adopted women nonetheless deserve a unique platform and discourse. The rationale for this perspective developed as a result of the primary research agenda focusing on the fact that adopted women experience natural birth during the course of their lives. They carry their own biological offspring in the womb for a nine month period that is counted daily, weekly and monthly. The very heartbeats of their own developing child echo in their reflections on infant abandonment. This prism is what led me to believe that there is still much to learn about the worlds of identity, physicality and emotion in adopted women who themselves have become mothers. Without doubt, the field of research will also gain much from qualitative study that sets its goal at exploring the experiences of identity fixing and fatherhood among adopted men in Israel.

As part of existential philosophy, there is clear consensus that because mankind has no fixed and frozen nature, it is destined to continually create itself, along the lines of: past has passed, the present is but the blink of an eye, and the future is yet to be. Philosophers relating to the experience of existence in the world of the absurd claimed that mankind was a pure event of being, but what – or who – mankind is cannot be determined through one singular event of coming into being. However, existential philosophers claimed that self-definition and the significance given to human existence are still to be found within the historical-realistic context, and only the absolute nature cannot be defined by Man, who is always able to choose one of an infinite array of reactions, interpret her or his life however she or he finds appropriate, become strengthened in endless ways, and accept or reject her or his own choices.

Certainly, choice and freedom are principles central to existential philosophy. The stance taken by existential philosophers relative to choice relates as a matter of course to the concept of freedom: there is no meaningful value to talk on choice and preference without assuming mankind's freedom. Therefore, most existential philosophers identify choice with freedom. In other words, being human means being free. For these philosophers, freedom is comprised of two conceptualities: *freedom from...*, and *freedom to...* The first relates to freedom from causal determinations, from nature and externally imposed enforcements. By contrast, the latter refers to the freedom, as an autonomy, to new self-creation and self-legislation. In the framework of *freedom to,* one is entitled to create the self within oneself, as appropriate to a system of rules and laws brought into being for that self (Golomb, 1990). This brief philosophical polemic arouses a quandary: do the issues of *freedom from...* and *freedom to...* exist for all, or is freedom a privilege for only those whose life histories are in their own hands? Paradoxically, it then becomes possible to complicate the issue further with another question: how can those whose life history is an unknown choose to free themselves from it? Existential philosophers go one step further and note that even in the life of the free man, there is a historical-realistic context.

In Rivkele Mondalek's *My Child,* she describes the start of her life as an adopted woman: "I came into the world as a refugee. No visa, no address. The tremendous love I received was and still is very meaningful, but does not have the power of healing the pain of desertion" (Mondalek, 2003). Emptiness and deficiency both appear in that very first feed bottle given to the adopted child at the outset of her or his life, they swaddle from the very beginning, they appear at the conceptual-rational level (details in one's genealogy and history of blood ties), and are no less important at the experiential-emotional level (the periods of time, from days to months, during which the soft touch of mother is absent), all of which Mondalek terms "the pain of desertion".

Research conducted by Malchiel in *Intention, Sensation and Emotion*, shows his awareness of the emotional echoes structuring mankind's consciousness. In Malchiel's opinion, the term "pain" encompasses both the public and disclosed, as well as the subjective and concealed:

> Phenomenal events are not necessarily events of the art of self-consciousness [...] they are simply there, in the consciousness, in their objective substance. Despite the subject not loading them with any particular significance or mental attunement, they are highly meaningful for that individual (Malchiel, 2001, pg. 194).[8]

The prism of pain, that "pain of desertion", finds its echoes in all the adopted women. The culture, values and norms (particularly in Israel which strongly encourages natality) beat out a clear message of mother love. An example can be

---

8   Malchiel, A. (2001). *Intention, sensation and emotion: Subjectivity and its philosophical forms of clarification.* Jerusalem: Magnes. (pg. 194). [in Hebrew].

found in Professor Ada Lampert's 1995 book, *The Evolution of Love*, where she describes mother love as a model of primary love:

> In life's evolutionary chain of events, from the first simple forms, the microbes, to the full range of complex life-forms currently existing at any time in this sequentiality, mother-love appeared as the primary love on this earth. Mother-love is the most basic of all loves ever developed within evolution, and is primary within the individual lives of each of us. The initial love we experience is that of the mother. This dual primacy turns it into a love model, the archetype for all other loves that we will ever come to know in the course of life. Later loves seemingly draw from that mother's love the materials needed to allow experiencing love. I refer to hormones, the nervous system, and the cerebral processes which recur in later loves as though they were mother-love (Lampert, 1995, pg. 37).

The vivid description offered by Lampert does not deal with the mothering instinct (a disputed term) in any way; it does not require or seek mothering commitment. The charm in her description derives chiefly from the simplicity of its natural order in Creation. Her description conceptualizes motherly love as a derivative of bringing forth life, as an operative connected like an umbilical cord to giving birth. But this loving naturalness, which encompasses the cycle of life and nurtures its beings, is emptied of content when we begin to discuss the experiences of adopted women: in the tangible and perceptible experience of women who were adopted as infants, there remains the eternal memory of abandonment in the earliest stages of life. The obviousness of being enveloped, cradled and touched are not part of the chronology of natural development for these adopted women. Furthermore, in accordance with adoption policy – pervasive almost worldwide – the birth mother who chooses to have her child adopted is required to waive her primary right to love. She is prohibited from caressing the newborn's skin, or hugging the child. She is not allowed to smell her newborn, or perform any act that may arouse a connection that will make future separation more difficult.[9] However, the presence of the adopting mother in the child's life may lead to the formation of a new definition of love. Indeed, it is interesting to see how, in another section of her book, Professor Lampert explained mother-love in mankind. That description far better demonstrates the perceived experience of love in the lives of adopted women:

> Love was invented by mammalian mothers needing to protect their newborn who are helpless, unable to maintain their own body temperature and open to dangers. Motherhood is commitment to assisting the young; the emotions of love and warmth accompanying motherhood are sourced in urge and fulfillment which provide the motivation for mothering (Lampert, 1995, pg. 23).

Between these two extremes, adopted women balance their conceptualizations of mother-love. Among themselves, they swim about, sometimes torn by the pain of loss and mourning, sometimes thankful for the love that is part of their lives. These polarized views of love may resurface as an unresolved equation when they themselves become

9   From an interview with Ms. Orna Hirschfeld and Ms. Devorah Shabtai, both of Child Services, held on 24 June 2009, Israel apparently has developed a different policy. Welfare representatives actually encourage the biological birther to perform some act that signifies separation and closure relative to the infant intended for adoption.

mothers. The two extremes are not unlike two steps taken in tight succession through the lives of adopted women. Lampert's two descriptions on the nature of a mother's love shed light on yet another polarity in the identity structure of adopted women: the tension between natural and cultural.

The experience of adoption, and especially closed adoption, binds natural and cultural in the adopted woman's conceptualization. The encounter between nature and culture contains the enigmatic, rattling the framework of "working on identity" and attempting to "establish identity" among adopted women. Every adopted woman's biography presents knowledge of a biological "shadow family". In the early stages of life, this family is perceived as a kind of archived entity, a vague presence in the unclear early biography. Yet despite being blurred and faint, this entity beats and rustles throughout all stages of life. At some point, usually at maturity and on reaching 18 years old, the curtain can be raised to reveal this "shadow entity". A dazzling shaft of light will expose the backdrop, the background narrative and the actors who were no more than a figment of imagination until this point in time. On occasion, the disparity experienced on opening the adoption file and contacting the biological family will be so great as to blind the adoptee into closing her eyes. For others, the curtain will rise for only an instant, letting no more than meager light through, leaving them yearning for more: in that very moment, of infinite passion and longing, the curtain will close once more before their very eyes. In parched voice, they will admit that information on their past is missing, or that they were not permitted for some or another reason to meet the biological family. Those fine cracks of discovery will leave them angry, frustrated, and chiefly, helpless. Others, having enacted all possible scenarios from every feasible angle in their minds, may conclude that it is simply too dangerous to raise a curtain that had been closed for some twenty years: these women choose to forego opening the adoption file and suspend the act indefinitely, continuing their lives alongside the experience of the "shadow entity" in their minds. Each and every one of them will find it hard to look inside that file; each and every one will need to be satisfied with fragments of knowledge, scraps of memory, ribbons of biography worked like the endless stitching and unraveling of patches – a patchwork blanket of identity.

Descriptions like these do not contradict the warm, loving presence and attention they received within their adoptive families. These descriptions take into account the presence of the adoptive family which courageously and indefatigably makes all efforts at filling the gaps, making whole that which was lacking, raising, providing, mediating and supporting, and much more. But for adopted women, this is simultaneously their deliverance and their tragedy; for how can one guiltlessly bemoan loss in the arms of the adoptive mother and father who do all possible for their child! From these depths practical solutions are formed that silence the pain. The women will develop understandings of allowed and forbidden, create clear boundaries of unification and separation, they will restrict their life's paths while ensuring there are bypass routes: their whole purpose is to manage conflicting comprehensions of reality, where the natural is absent and the cultural is extant. These are also the materials with which they will weave their couplehood relationships, and with which they embroider their views on childhood, maturity, entitlement and parenthood when they themselves become biological mothers.

The Research

The starting point for this study is an empiric perception accompanied by an intuitive sensation that the voices of adopted women have not been sufficiently heard in the framework of qualitative methodology, which emphasizes the phenomenological in the feminine narrative. Existing studies are founded on the patronizing approach that adopted women must be spoken about and spoken for. In the said studies, they are not referred to as "adopted women" but as "adopted girls", as though they have never been in an exclusive partnership, and therefore are public property. They are repeatedly adopted: by researchers examining their adaptation, their psychological and physical qualifications, and their spiritual, emotional and mental capabilities. But they themselves have remained silent.

During my study, I discovered that the interviewees share the experience of silencing, which they describe as a reality sometimes enforced on them or which may constitute a strategy employed in the management of their decisions and choices. They stay silent when facing the patrons of the institution which mediated between them and their adoption files. They stayed silent out of respect for their adoptive parents. They stayed silent, too, as a practical solution to protecting the secrecy of the biological birth parents. This silence enabled the various experts to create platforms which spoke on their behalf, and employed terms such as "for the child's sake", "for the child's protection", "the child's best interest" and so on. Their silence occasionally leaves them without gender, and at other times refers to them as "girls" even though they are long since married, have given birth and become mothers in their own right. Even when women did take up the reins and decide to have their voices heard, these were isolated, individual voices, of the woman "alone in the watch tower", investing lone effort.

Comprehending this, I felt that the very act of recruiting interviewees might become an impossible objective. Discretion, immunity and ethics were all well-entrenched fortifications on the way to my encounter with the interviewees. Nonetheless, the first stage, based on a snowball sampling, proved to me that beyond the adopted women with whom I was personally acquainted, there are many others who know or have met an adopted woman at least once in their lives. Activating go-betweens, I made approaches geared at "outing" adopted women still "in the closet". These requests were accompanied by long days of expectation, as behind-the-scenes clarification was conducted with the adopted women.

During this phase, I was struck by an interesting basic premise presented by my 'mediators': that this was a sensitive issue and the potential interviewees must be approached with trepidation and respect. This approach opened a Pandora's box of commonly held beliefs and stigmas relative to adopted women. When these mediators came back to me with their responses, I heard the wonder in their voices over the fact that almost all the potential interview candidates approached were very glad to participate. At this point, it seemed that the potential interviewees and I agreed on one matter very clearly: it was high time the women's voices were heard. Another avenue through which I was able to locate interviewees was instrumental use of online forums and communities. On receiving the agreement of the forum managers to run a notice seeking interviewees, adopted women themselves initiated contact. I also attended a frontal meeting with members of an online forum, where

I presented my study and need for additional interviewees. Cooperation was total. Women offered to describe, in fine detail, their experiences as adopted girls and women. Fairly quickly I realized that the initial agenda with which I had set out into the field of research, that is, interviews geared at exploring the experience of transition to motherhood in adopted women, was too narrow and inadequate.

This understanding surfaced during the course of interviews where the women's narratives overflowed into spheres of wider identity coping, including childhood, adolescence, opening the adoption file, meeting with the biological birth mother, and more. At certain times, it seemed as though the adopted women themselves wished to take maximum advantage of the platform offered them and kick wildly at the blanket of secrecy wound about them. At other times, I felt that they might be making tendentious use of me in closing accounts with absentee mothers, fathers who disappeared, and the impossible situations in which they found themselves after opening their adoption files.

By now I realized that immunity and ethics must constitute the cornerstones that delineate the outlines of the study. An additional insight centered on the fact that reflecting on the transition to biological motherhood was only the tip of the iceberg, and that deep within the unseen, submerged part of that iceberg throbbed complex emotional thoughts which often could be recalled from the early age of 4 years old. Finally, I reached a decision: as part of my commitment to feminist research, or at the very least, as part of my commitment to the initial premise that it is vital to have the voice of adopted women heard, I would need to free myself up for expanded work on research. As such, interviews planned for limited time frames of between one to two hours were allowed to deviate significantly into much longer time frames, even up to five hours' duration.

My explanation for this exception derived from at least two reasons: one was the unequivocal need displayed by the women themselves to talk and break that mantle of silence. The other was the manner in which the interview was conducted. Every interview began with a "trustworthiness test" directed from the interviewee towards me. They wanted to know my story. In this sense, my being adopted proved itself as the channel by which I gained what is known in feminist research as "active listening" and rapport during the interview. In the course of this process, the significance of ethics, discretion and protection of the interviewees' personal privacy surfaced yet again. These aspects are translated into the way in which I chose to present the research findings, that is: no real names are mentioned, whether of the interviewees, of biological or adoptive mothers, or any other persons having meaningful roles in the interviewees' lives. Although feminist research is set up for a system of pseudonyms which encompass not only first but also family names, for this study I gave expanded consideration to the sensitivity of the content and chose an aware strategy that even avoids pseudonyms or any description that may directly or indirectly identify the interviewees. Some interviews were audio recorded with the interviewee's permission, while others were only hand written.

All the interviewees fulfilled the socio-demographic status: 15 women born in Israel and adopted via inland adoption. The interviewees ranged in age from 20 to 43 years old. Their education ranged from 12 to 17 years of study. The interviewees live in different locations throughout Israel. Of the 15, 12 are mothers and only three have yet to experience motherhood.

The following chapters will present the interviewees' own descriptions of significant points along the axis of their lives. The concepts that the women themselves formed, which they describe as milestones in formulating their worlds of identity and emotion, are examined by them through the lens of being adopted girls and women. Their descriptions are accompanied by theoretical discussion, from the perspective of research exploring adoption.

Chapter One

"On Being a Suspect Little Girl"

The Experience of Adoption in Earliest Childhood – Content related to Desertion, Belonging, and Acceptance

> *Communication is of utmost importance, and central to the development and functioning of humans throughout their lives. Separation in general, and death in particular, constitute a threat for mankind. (Witztom, 2004, pg.53)*

In the framework of interviews I held with adopted women, two main spheres of coping typical of earliest childhood surfaced.[1] These areas of coping deal with (1) fear of abandonment in early childhood; and (2) early deliberations over familial and social inclusion, differentiation and difference.

1. "If you go away, I'll die": Desertion Anxiety in Early Childhood.

In the WHO [World Health Organization] report of 1951, prepared by John Bowlby who was requested to provide recommendations concerning the mental health of homeless children, he wrote:

---

1   The term "earliest childhood" refers to ages 3 to 10 years old.

[57]

> We believe that the most vital state for good mental health
> is that the infant and young child should experience a warm,
> intimate, and continuous relationship with his mother (or
> permanent mother substitute) in which both find satisfaction
> and enjoyment (Bowlby, 1951, pg. 13).

Bowlby's pioneering work, *Attachment and loss*, led eventually to the development of Attachment Theory. Certainly in theoretical frameworks, attachment has been given expansive attention as far as the negative consequences of detaching (that is, separation of) the child from the parents at a young age (Bowlby, 1973). Attachment Theory contributed to the field of research in raising awareness of the importance of attachment among children to a central care-giving figure, and the importance of the relationship formed between adult and child.

Alongside these claims, however, researchers of the early 1980s began claiming that Bowlby focused too specifically on the mother-child relationship, and it was clear that children could attach to more than one care-giver (Phillips, 1989; Rutter, 1981). These studies found that a supportive environment can constitute a compensatory substitute, or at the least, reduce the negative effect created following abandonment. Researchers conducting a comprehensive psychological study of children adopted by Dutch parents claimed that this question is even more critical in the context of adoptees. The researchers ask whether the children separated from parents at earliest infancy can succeed in bonding to an adoptive parent; and further, whether the adoptive mother who has not experienced the pregnancy and birth can succeed in bonding fully with the infant (Juffer & Rosenboom, 1997).

Certainly studies conducted on the basis of Bowlby's (1973) attachment theory found that children adopted prior to the age of 6 months experienced outbursts of crying when the mother left the room, and refused to detach from her when she returned to their side. By contrast, infants adopted after the age of 6 months manifested real resistance towards the mother, or alternately, stubborn clinginess. These infants, on arriving at their adoptive homes, also displayed behaviors indicating developmental regression (Yarrow & Goodwin, 1973). Numerous studies exploring issues of attachment among adoptees (Ainsworth, Blehar, Waters & Wall, 1978) dealt with issues of attachment, confidence and lack of confidence in early suckling-aged infants, but did not relate to how adopted adults translate and conceptualize their experience of earliest childhood. Juffer and Rosenboom (1997) presented this problem and explored the issues quantitatively.

In the current study, I seek to give a special place to the earliest childhood memories of adopted women. Through this avenue, I hoped to clarify core experiences of adoption at kindergarten age with them. One theme predominant in the semi-structured interviews with these women was their fear of abandonment throughout earliest childhood. Most interestingly, and unrelated to the age at which they were adopted, all the interviewees described their deep fear of the adopted parent leaving. Below is the description of a woman adopted at the age of two weeks:

> I experienced tremendous trauma, real fear of abandonment. I wasn't prepared for my parents to leave me even for a moment. When they went out, I was anxious until they returned. The whole time, I'd be pondering the question of how to take care of my two sisters (two biological daughters born to the adoptive mother after the interviewee was adopted) should they not return anymore. Once it was really exaggerated: my

sisters sat on the sofa, younger than me by three and four years respectively, and I cried incessantly, unable to stop crying.

Later in the interview, this woman remembers another event:

> I refused to participate in after-school enrichment groups, because the whole time I'd be anxious about whether my father would be waiting downstairs. I joined an organ playing class once, a very small group, and I was about 10 years old. The teacher was very pleasant, and only a few of us remained in the class eventually, perhaps four of us. The teacher always related to me nicely, but I left this class too, in tears, because I decided that perhaps the teacher is being so nice because she's my (biological) mother. I remember leaving the lesson in the middle and running home in tears, and asking my adoptive mother: *Is it possible that the teacher's my real mother?*

These excerpts clearly show abandonment anxiety mixed with content relative to the issues of biological mother identity. Perhaps the very present fear described by the interviewee in that situation was drawn from the narrative of early adoption, and the integration unites content of abandonment in early childhood with the fear of abandonment of later years.

Eliezer Witzom (2004), a professor of psychology, in *Soul, mourning and bereavement*, explained that:

> A child tries to overcome detachment anxiety through unification or closeness. When the individual matures, the main need of closeness is found at the intra-psychic level, the unconscious. The main wish is to become close to the internalized representations. It is known that a state of loss

often creates an encounter between the need to come closer to the individual her- or himself, and the *need to come closer to her or his representation.* Often this is a very tangible need, and causes the adult to return to various modes of conduct connected with the deceased, sometimes even emulating the deceased's behavior (Witztom, 2004, pg. 52).

Cross-referencing Witztom's views with the description provided by the interviewee indicates that this process can occur among children conceptualizing the experience of abandonment. It seems that the interviewee perceives the image of her music teacher as the tangible representation of the biological birth mother, an experience that causes her to leave the lesson in tears. Witztom (2004) further states that:

The desperateness of need to connect with the close individual who has disappeared from the life of close kin creates the equally desperate desire to connect to that individual despite her or his non-existence. This kind of behavior is not especially effective; therefore it is necessary to acknowledge the new reality and the disorganization expressing the pressuring situation formed, and later even the temporary sense of disrupted mood, sadness and longing (Witztom, 2004, pg. 53).

In another instance an interviewee, adopted at the age of 3 months, tells me:

Every time my mother would go downstairs to buy something at the grocer's, I'd sit on the floor by the huge window overlooking the road. To get to the grocery store, my mother had to cross the road. I'd sit all cramped up waiting for her to cross the road. It was very important to me that she'd cross the road without being run over. I'd wait there beneath the window until she returned. Every time, I was sure that this time she'd be run over, that this time she wouldn't return home, and from that thought alone I'd burst into tears.

From the interviewees' descriptions, abandonment anxiety afflicts them all, and is not dependent on the age at which they were adopted. The next excerpt demonstrates that not only does the deserting figure have a mental image, but that this representation exists relative to the experience of abandonment. Similarly, an interviewee adopted at 10 months old claims:

We were in the Kol-Bo Shalom [department store] and my mother put me and my brother [adopted, and older by a year] in the play area upstairs. We played and played, and then she came over, and picked up my brother and hugged him tightly. She said something that I don't recall now, ah, probably that she was going to buy drinks or something, and she's leaving me in the play room. I got hysterical, crying, screaming, throwing myself on the floor. I remember the image of them both going together and I'm looking at them. I was sure a million percent that they were leaving me there, and going away. I felt like a lost child, alone in the world. Immediately the announcement system was activated and my mother was called to return. When she came back, I remember telling her, *if you go away from me again, I'll die.*

I wished to explore the question of how the interviewees themselves explained these sensations. I was interested in clarifying *how, in their view,* the abandonment anxiety that they described took hold. I directed the question particularly towards interviewees adopted when already several weeks old. One explanation provided by an interviewee adopted at the age of 6 weeks, was the following:

> I thought about this. It doesn't make any difference how many days you were in the hospital, or in the children's home, the nurses would be constantly changing. And what does a baby need? Ah? Stability. The morning shift nurse isn't the night shift nurse, and in the morning there are a lot of different nurses, think about it a bit, every second there's a different touch, going from one set of hands to the next. You don't even see a permanent face. For us, from the age of zero, there's no closeness, no fixed figure. We were never breastfed, never connected to a heartbeat, we never smelled the smell of mother, we never felt her body. For sure that's connected with our fear; until finally, once there's a permanent, single figure, it's important to us that she stays very close by. And also, in my view, it's connected to the fact that afterwards, we're always running between different people trying to endear ourselves … and everyone's trying to adopt us again, and again. The adopted child is a public child.

Indeed, in studies by Senecky, Diamond, Sapir and Inbar (2003), the claim is made that in tests run in British institutions during the 1960s, it was found that up to the age of two years old, the potentially-adoptable child encounters some 20 different care-givers; up to the age of 4 years old, 40 care-givers; and up to 8 years old, the child has already encountered 80 care-givers. In their view, physical contact between infant and care-giver is generally no more than functional, diminished to the time needed to change diapers and feed the child, and physical contact beyond those needs is rare. The most frequently experienced problems, as pointed to by the researchers, concern creating social connections and emotional stability. The researchers seek to relate to these situations as manifesting post traumatic stress disorder.

In work conducted by Schore (1996) emphasis was also placed on the influence of touch on the infant's and child's development. Schore claimed that the mother-infant dyad represents the process of non-verbal attachment between the individual's private self and another's private self and will have influence throughout the individual's life. In other words, this process is basic to the child's development and represents non-verbal body-mind communication. It is vital to creating relationships with closeness, including the care-giving relationship. Schore noted that the transference of emotion, as surfacing in his work, represents right brain reciprocity, which he claimed is the tool for transferring attachment norms, a tool based primarily on senses, physical touch and emotion or, in other words, is not based on cognition. From these premises it seems that experiences having a sensory physical nature constitute an intimate and vital process to attachment. It is possible that the absence of the physical-sensory dimension in earliest infancy unconsciously contributes to those anxieties described by the intervieweesLike a silk thread, the experience of fear of abandonment runs through all the narratives provided by these adopted women, no matter how old they were when adopted. The predominant sense among the women is that early childhood is characterized by the lack of what Mahler (1975) termed "object constancy". In her opinion, during the second individuation phase which commences at 4 years old, detachment should begin to develop in the mother-child relationship. This state arises because the first individuation phase, beginning at suckling age, ought to provide the baby with sufficient independence and confidence through the very physical-concrete presence of the mother, and by virtue of knowing that the mother is the constant supplier of the infant's needs. It is a vital stage in enabling physical separation from the mother; that very separation is enabled by virtue of object constancy (Mahler, Pine & Bergman, 1975). Possibly this explanation becomes underscored when relating to adopted children, in that the absence of a stable figure in earliest babyhood contributes unconsciously to the refusal to separate from such a figure during infancy and early childhood once that figure has eventually entered the infant's life through adoption.

Another explanation of interest can be found in the literature dealing with adoptive parents and how they read their adopted child. Ainsworth (et al., 1978) relates to the interaction between adopted child and adoptive parents. Researchers feel it is necessary to conduct close-up examinations of the scope of awareness in adoptive parents to the special needs of the adopted child. Their view states that because the adoptive parents are not familiar with the child from the moment of birth, adoptive parents may experience real difficulty at least during the initial stages of adoption, in reading and understanding the child's emotional signals. The early phase of adoption, then, is also a period of adaptation and learning, only after which Bowlby's (1973) attachment can occur.

Looking at how these ideas cross-reference with the findings of the current study, it seems that the issue of adoptive age (week/s or month/s) is not relevant to the difficulties created later, as an additional factor in structuring the sense of stability is related to the dynamics developing between the adoptive parent and the adopted child, and the child's absorption into the adoptive family home.

2. "Children aren't found in garbage cans" –
Belonging and alienation, the fine line between
adoptees and everyone else

Elizabeth L. Rompf (1993) set out to track the public stances of "the average Joe" in relation to "open adoption". In the course of her research, she asked her survey participants a range of questions designed to clarify views held by the general public concerning adoptees in general, and open adoption in particular. The findings of her study indicate that several basic assumptions are the source of the generally held views on the adoptee's position and emotions. She found, for example, that adoptees are perceived as persons who will be preoccupied throughout their lives with questions relating to their biological parents, and will therefore undoubtedly seek their biological parents: 86% of the 640 individuals questioned answered positively on whether adoptees would want to open their adoption files. In addition, the overwhelming majority of participants, 70% of the 640 individuals questioned, expressed unwillingness to adopt a child or even consider the idea of adoption. Rompf concludes in her study that the general public predominantly believes biological parenthood to be of greater importance. As a result, adoptees are considered persons who would obviously want to open the adoption file, and the adoptive parent is even expected to assist the adopted child in doing so (ibid). Nonetheless, I would suggest that yet another conclusion is alluded to and surfaces from Rompf's research: adoption is perceived as an unnatural situation, which is not preferable to biological parenthood, and this paradox can only be settled when the adoptee seeks her or his biological roots.

As part of the current study, interviewees were asked to

describe events they recalled from their earliest childhood which reflect on the issue of adoption. From their narratives it becomes absolutely clear that the attitude towards adoption is negative, as discovered in their first social encounter with the children at kindergarten, or the extended family. The experience seems characterized by the feeling that at this inter-social stage, they are exposed to the drawing of a fine line separating biological children from adoption children: the message conveyed to the adoptees is of negative context, relating to "you" and "us". This is how one interviewee describes the situation:

> I came to kindergarten one morning; I was about 3 years old. By this stage I already knew I was adopted, and positive aspects were always connected to the idea of adoption. My mother would say that we'd adopt the teddy together, and together we'd hug it tight. In other words, in our home, adoption held a very positive significance. So in short, I came to kindergarten and another little girl stood there, who was my best friend, called Hanit [a pseudonym]. She stood there, her feet apart, and wouldn't let me through the doorway. She stood there, asking me, *did you know that your mother found you in the garbage can?* I didn't have a clue what she was referring to. Now I can't even remember how I felt. My mother told me that I came home and asked her, *what, did you find me in the rubbish?* And she answered, *Children aren't found in garbage cans. Tell her she's silly, children like you come from the heart.* The next day, the kindergarten teacher told my mother that when I arrived at the kindergarten, I waited until she [the friend] came, and said to her, *Silly, children aren't found in the garbage. Children are from the heart.*

Another interviewee presents a similar anecdote:

> It was really toughest for me in primary school. I was constantly being jibed and bothered because of the adoption. I told one girlfriend, and she took advantage of it all the time. She'd say to me, *if you don't give me this or that, I'll tell everyone.* It made no difference what I did, in the end she chose to tell. And the children really harassed me. I remember once a social lesson was held specially for my sake, the teacher explaining about adoption, and you know, about being tolerant, not bullying, all that ... in the recess, one boy from my class came up to me and said, *I'm not laughing at you because you're situation's miserable. You haven't got parents.*

In research conducted by Deacon (1997), analyzing adoption through the family life cycle theory, she indeed states that the kindergarten and primary school stages are critical for adoptees: in any event, they begin questioning a range of issues related to the reasons behind being abandoned, their relationship relative to their biological parents, and the knowledge that there exists, at least technically, a double set of parent figures. Thus the descriptions provided by the interviewees indicate how the adoptees' immanent questions quickly become questions directed right at the adoptees themselves. In another case, the issue of inclusiveness surfaces interestingly from within the adoptee's close family, as related by an interviewee:

> I encountered the ugly aspect of adoption, actually, through my family members. When it happened, I was about 7 years old, something like Grade 2. In our family, the differences are very noticeable. You could see clearly that I didn't belong – my color, height, appearance. We went downstairs, my cousin and I, and then a friend of my cousin saw us, and asked her, *who's that?* and she answered, *that's my cousin, she's adopted.*

Q: What actually offended you about this?

A: She didn't say anything bad, or insulting, but I felt that the way she defined me as adopted was as though that wasn't natural.

Another of the interviewees had this to say:

When I was around 10 years old, we lived in a two-family home. On the other side of the joint wall lived a family comprised of a mother and two daughters. This mother fought with the whole neighborhood, and always followed me to see what I was up to. In her mind, I was a "suspicious child". One day she heard my mother and me arguing. She waited for me in the shared yard, watching. When I got a little way from the house, she approached and said very loudly, *if that's how you scream at your mother, in the end you won't have a mother.*

Q: How did you react?

A: I don't remember what I said. I just remember being insulted, and very, very panicked. I went back home with a lot of questions about my life. She wouldn't let me go until I promised her I'd be a good girl. I stood there and told her that I promise it wouldn't happen again, and she didn't understand what I was saying. When I went home, this went round and round in my mind, and eventually I told my mother, who told me not to pay her any attention, that she's not very smart.

One of the most prominent and recurring expressions voiced by this interviewee throughout the interview with her was "suspicious child". The interviewee described the circumstances in which she felt like a "suspicious child". I attempted to clarify just what she meant by that phrase:

My whole childhood and adolescence was colored by the experience of "being suspicious". There's something about being adopted that keeps you always under scrutiny – am I really a good daughter? Will I really be nice when my parents are elderly? And just who is that odd girl with the mysterious story? Who is she, that adopted one? You know what, even as a mother I felt as though there were people asking themselves these kinds of questions: if she herself is adopted, how can she be a good mother?

These descriptions need to be reviewed in comparison with research literature on the subject of adoption. Analyzing adoption according to family life cycle theory, researchers found that in early childhood, in addition to the social environment which raises both direct and indirect questions on adoption, the adoptive parents convey a message to the adopted child of disparity between natural and cultural, in the form of "us" and "you".[2] These messages appear, according to Deacon (1997) chiefly when the child's behavior is normative, that is, as part of normal development and childhood pranks. Often, as apparent from the research, many parents relate to these negative phenomena with explanations that refer to the child's genetic makeup: "Many times, the child's bad behaviors will be rationalized as the child's bad biological genes."[3]

Situations such as these create emotional conflict, as the adopted child is also often in a state of testing the degree to which she or he is accepted by the adoptive family.

2   As cited in Rosenberg, E.B. (1992). The adoption life cycle. New York: Free Press
3   As cited in Deacon, S. (1997). Inter country adoption and the family life cycle. The American Journal of Family Therapy, Vol. 25 (3), pg. 251

Another interviewee stresses how, even when much older, relatively simple events are scrutinized as though through a magnifying glass made of mainstreaming and inclusiveness:

> It'll probably sound stupid to you, but there was a time when it was fashionable to wear men's clothing, and I took my father's button front shirt. My father went nuts, and forbade me from ever touching his things. I was sure that was because I wasn't his biological daughter, and that he was afraid I'd sweat it in and leave a strange body odor.

Similar to this is the description by an interviewee coping with the issue of bath towels not shared by all the family members:

> It's nothing so serious, but it's engraved on my mind. It was summer holidays, and two female cousins were guests at our house. We took showers, and my mother brought clean towels, one for each of us. When we were done washing, one of the cousins noticed the towels, that usually there's one for each person in the household, and then she said, *At our place everyone uses the same towel. What's this? Why has everyone got a different towel, are you repulsed by each other? Maybe it's because you're adopted?*

The sense of being alien is imprinted into the body, touches the body and returns to it, while at the same time it seeps into the identity experience of otherness and separateness. What the previous interviewee termed "suspicious child", can take an indirect and more cunning form, as described by this interviewee who did not know until the age of 17 that she was adopted:

My brother and I were the attractions in the family, and we never understood why. At every family event, all the relatives would come to us and stand at our table and talk with us. At first I thought it was because we're special or wonderful. At that time, I still didn't know we're adopted. Only when I was older, and knew I was adopted, did I understand that they came to look at us, like monkeys at the zoo, as though, *Hey, let's look at what these adopted kids have achieved.*

It is interesting to note how encounters within the expanded family serve as the basis for emotional venting towards the adopted daughter; or as one interviewee called them, "events for settling accounts":

Before my parents adopted my brother and I, it was clear to everyone, especially in the family, that my mother would bequeath everything she had to my cousins because she herself had no child. My mother told me that her sister and niece came to visit her, even before we were born, and the little niece said to my mother, *Mother, I'll get Aunt's ring when she dies.* Later we were adopted, and of course [leaving them everything] became unrealistic. But here's the thing: it seems that's not so, and they've borne [us] a grudge for taking the place that could have been theirs. At my brother's bar mitzvah, there was a cake decorated with a book, and my brother and I cut the cake, and each of us took a piece. The cousins stood next to us, and after cutting two or three slices, they said to us, *Enough, that's enough, you've taken plenty. It's not yours anymore, it's ours.*

As understood from these descriptions, the senses of alienation and otherness, of difference and separateness, start to manifest from the outset of adoptees' lives. Agents of these messages are many and varied: people in the neighborhood, an acquaintance, relatives, friends from kindergarten, and even the parents themselves without any awareness of what they are doing. As the adoptees become more familiarly acquainted with separateness, they develop 'sensors' which constitute a kind of magnifier through which everything related with identity is judged. This is the description offered by another interviewee:

> I had a neighbor, a commander in the army, who thought he was really intelligent. When I was school age, he said to me one day, *You, let's see what comes of you eventually,* and I answered, *You'll see, I'll go far.* From that stage on, I think, everything I did was to prove myself. That's to say, the adoption was always somewhere there, even though from my point of view, I wanted people to look at me as a person in my own right, not only as a mysterious, adopted child.

Early familiarization with the experience of otherness fine-hones new mechanisms of awareness. Their sensitivity is accelerated during adolescence when questions relating to identity are formulated in a more complex manner and include attitudes towards the biological mother, and other questions concerning biological issues in particular, and genetics in general.

Chapter Two

Adolescence – A Patched Identity

"I embroider an identity made up of patches"

The desire to find meaning in life is a primal, driving force in mankind. Our need to mediate is a primary force rather than any "secondary intellectual" arm of instinctive urges. The need to mediate is unique and idiosyncratic in that only the individual her- or himself needs and can fulfill this desire: only in this way does it become clothed in meaning that can fill the person's desire to mediate ... which means not only elevation of the being per se, but that presence that faces being (Victor Frankl, [1970], 2001, pgs. 119-121).

In this chapter, I will explore the processes and content of the body, identity and emotion as these appear in the experiences of adopted adolescents. The literature dealing with adolescents shows a predominant approach that views adolescence as inherently containing dramatic changes. The boundaries of the age range termed "adolescent" by researchers is from 11 to 19 years old, and is also known as "the teens" (Rice & Dolgin, 2007). However, in recent generations, far-reaching changes have begun to filter through and currently, some researchers define adolescence as spreading over a far longer term. The relevant studies claim that adolescence actually starts at 8 years old, and only ends at around 20 or 21. No matter what the actual range, adolescence is described in the literature as the period that sees the greatest scope of change in the individual's physical, emotional and identity characteristics.

The first noticeable change during adolescence appears in the *body*, occurring in hormones and physical appearance and related to voice, height, and sexual organs. A more interesting finding, however, is the fact that these changes are chiefly characterized by the fact that the basis of comparison between the adolescent and her or his friends ceases to exist, as each adolescent experiences these changes at different rates. In addition, the physical changes are typified by lack of proportionality: in males, sexual organs may change at a disproportionate rate to changes in height, for example. Psychologists studying the physical aspects of adolescence claim that these two facets – the absence of comparison with others, and disproportionate bodily changes – arouse the sense of lack of control, which in turn increases anxiety. In counseling given to parents of adolescents, the message is often conveyed that in order to cope with "body anxiety", it is worth explaining to the adolescent that these changes will eventually cease, and the disparities will even out as growth continues. The intuitive statements that parents discussing these issues with their children might say are: "I also experienced changes like these in my body", or "I only grew taller after I was 14 years old", and so on.

In the current context, then, an interesting issue surfaces which is unique and prominent in the discourse on adopted children. In the framework of closed adoptions in Israel, the adoptive parents have no information at all on the biological parents. The Child Services, mediators on all adoption issues, avoids providing too much detail of a physiological nature when transferring the child to the adoptive parents (this is true for all children other than those with pathologies, health issues, genetic issues, etc). Thus, when the adopted child experiences the physical changes typical of adolescence, the adoptive parent is left helplessly facing the adolescent's questions about her or his body. Alongside dilemmas of body which the adopted child and the adoptive parents must absorb, additional psycho-emotional issues surface.

Deacon (1997) related to these aspects, stating that in the life of the adopted child, the physical changes in the body arouse real drama as they shape the future adult. The adoptee is left perplexed over similarities and differences, as closed adoption prevents the biological parents and the child from having contact and conveying information concerning the child's biological factors.

Indeed, researchers studying adolescence also relate to the complex psycho-emotional developments typical of that age range. During adolescence, issues related to the narrative on "the story of sequential identity development" surface in the adolescent's life. Anthony Giddens (1991) claimed that an inseparable part of the process of embedding identity involves the individual's ability to grasp this narrative: in other words, permanent themes which appear in fixed sequentiality in a person's life create a steadfast basis for structuring that individual's identity. Clearly, then, the adopted adolescent's sequential narrative is an impossibility, since from the outset of her or his life, multiple issues remain unresolved until the adoption file is opened. Added to that is the fact that adolescence is characterized by exploring the concepts of life and death, and the fear of mortality begins to expand. This argument can also be examined under the spotlight of the adoption experience: for the adopted child, the start of her or his life is an unknown, an enigma: how much more so the issue of death, in that closed adoption also closes access to information on blood ties and genetic illnesses.

Then there is the issue of devaluation of the parents'

position in the adolescent's life. Such devaluation may derive from many sources: such as the adolescent finding parents' diaries, or old letters, or information on genetics and genealogies. This kind of material turns the parents into "flesh and blood", causing disappointment and criticism in the adolescent towards the parents. During this stage, the natural distancing from the parent causes the adolescent to seek new bases of intimacy, usually found by connecting more closely with the peer group. These new, intimate ties create the sense of cooperation, closeness and comprehension. However, the next question surfacing is how adopted adolescents can formulate intimate circles when they are so focused on one, central issue: whether to confide their adopted status in that close and closed social circle. The next sections will delve into three dimensions of issues typical of female adolescents:

1. Experiences of body;
2. Experiences of identity;
3. Experiences of emotion.

I will also explore one additional theme which surfaced in the course of analyzing the findings; this theme deals with the issue of adolescence –

4. The absence of adolescent rebellion among adopted female adolescents

1. "What's in my blood that connects me with someone else?": Experiences of Body in Adolescence

The literature refers to adolescence as an age focused intensively on body. The adolescent is preoccupied with issues of similar and dissimilar between her or his body and that of others in the peer group in the broader social space. Adolescence is also typified by physical asymmetry of body, so that some body parts develop and clearly indicate physical maturity while others have yet to reach maturation. This disharmony, claim the researchers, gives rise to feelings of confusion, anxiety and fear relative to the body. It seems, then, that these contexts develop in somewhat unexpected and distinctive forms in relation to the adopted adolescent. From the narratives that the research interviewees described, the central experience representing adolescence for them is the awakening of questions concerning physical inclusiveness, similarity and genetics, rather than anxiety over the changing body. Apparently, the bodily changes give rise to concerns based on "Who do I look like?" However, the uniquely frustrating question for adoptees is that issues of physiological similarity remain unanswered, and cause strong emotions of frustration deriving chiefly from their inability to access those answers, leaving them constantly in the dark. One of the interviews contains this description:

> I remember constantly asking myself throughout adolescence, obsessively, who do I look like? What is there in my blood that connects me to someone else? A lot of questions of identity surfaced. Where did I come from? What did my mother look like? Sometimes, when I took the bus, I would ask myself: Could my mother be right here? Maybe among all these faces, she's sitting here? I asked myself things like: Who am I emulating when I make my choices? With my behavior?

A similar description is given by another interviewee:

> When I reached adolescence, the questions started: Why was I

the one to be deserted? What, was I so terrible? I asked myself: Who am I? What's my ethnicity? Do I have siblings? I directed these questions to my parents, too, and they would answer with brevity: *They weren't able to raise you, that's all.*

An interesting finding surfacing in many of the interviews indicates a focus on body arising when the social environment directs the adopted teen's attention to issues such as her being similar to/reminiscent of some other teen/woman:

When people would approach me and say, *You know, there's someone who really looks like you,* or something like, *Do you have a sister living in Tel Aviv? In Jerusalem?* or other remarks like these, I'd get all involved, start interrogating the person asking these questions: *Where does she live? Who are her parents?* As though I was trying to grasp every wisp of information that may remove the haziness from my life.

What is perceived as virtually marginal to biological children becomes the starting point for a line of sleuthing in the experiences of adopted teens. However, reality is such that these lines of questioning usually end up providing no answers. Even when the adopted teen does succeed in gaining a little information, this new data is accompanied by its own bundle of questions:

I returned from the overseas delegation, where I was constantly being told that I look as though I come from Italy, I must be Italian. Every time this surfaces, I feel as though I must fabricate against my will. If I say what my adoptive parents' origins are, then those remarks are made irrelevant because, in fact, they are not me, at least not in the ethnic sense. I had no information about my biological family at that stage, so what the *** am I supposed to say? In short, with all the turmoil it caused, I decided when I got home to start badgering my parents again. I remember they were lying in bed, and I came tearfully to them and absolutely begged them, *Tell me, just tell me, if I'm from Italy.* They looked at each other and didn't answer me. But I didn't let up: *I'm always being told that I look as though I'm from Italy, please, just tell me, because for sure I'm not from Poland, like you are. Please, just tell me.* I begged them like that for a long time, until eventually my mother told me: *Your biological mother is of Moroccan descent.*

The interviewee then told me how this new information not only did not resolve the issue, but caused a new set of questions to burn inside, without any responses:

As soon as they said "Moroccan", I started to cry out of sheer excitement. At last! I know something! Something very small, but at least it's something. I belong to an ethnic group, and that greatly reduced the scope of ethnicities to which I'd compare myself. And then I started to bombard them with questions, because I was left in hospital, apparently, due to being unhealthy, and there were all kinds of tests I still needed. So I started asking them about my health. I asked them if she was ill, what illness she had, you know, I was riding the wave of their beginning to "let the cat out of the bag", but my parents kept saying they don't know, they swore to me that beyond this [information], they didn't know anything else.

The interviewees' descriptions indicate a reality where the trivial, from the viewpoint of children living with their biological parents, becomes a complicated experience for adopted daughters. Attempts at investigating and clarifying the most fundamental facts of their existence are repelled by the adoptive parents' lack of knowledge. At this point, a very fascinating process occurs, where the body seems to create its own "body narrative", intended to fill out the missing parts of the puzzle. This curious process appears in the narratives of three interviewees.

> Every Purim[1] I'd draw a large beauty mark on my left check. I've no idea why I did it, but I was very pedantic about doing it just about each time. It made no difference what I dressed up as – an angel, a clown, a fairy – I always added that mark on my face [pointed out, but not detailed here - ethical discretion]. When I opened the adoption file and met [name of biological source], I was shocked to discover that [name] had a beauty mark in that exact place on the face.

Here, I emphasize that the interviewee repeated her statement that until she opened the adoption file, she had never seen a photograph of the biological relative referred to, nor ever been exposed to that person in any way, but some inexplicable body experience led her to drawing the beauty mark on her face. This phenomenon also appeared in the description provided below by another interviewee:

> From a very young age, I loved braids. I would go to school with braids, and even in high school loved to braid my hair all the time. In fact, even when it wasn't fashionable to have braids, I had them. When I opened the adoption file, and after meeting with the social worker several times, the social worker who sat beside me opened the conversation by saying: *Your biological mother came here when pregnant* [description by

---

1   Jewish festival replete with fancy-dress costumes for all ages.

the interviewee]. *She entered the room, her hair in a long braid* [description by interviewee]. The moment she described [my mother], I started to cry.

These experiences, which I would term "body intelligence", appear in the interview with yet another adopted woman:

Ever since I was young, I had a recurring dream. I would dream that someone was changing the color of my skin and my eyes. This dream repeated itself many times. As you see, I am dark-skinned, as are my parents, so I couldn't understand where this dream sprang from, and why it would repeat itself so frequently. When I opened the adoption file and met my biological mother, I realized she perfectly matched the figure of my dreams.

Just what is this phenomenon, then, through which adopted daughters conceptualize body image against biological sources without any prior knowledge of these sources? Is this perhaps an unconscious effort at arranging a biological identity on the basis of the endless probing of "Who do I look like?" In fact, this need appears in the work of various researchers studying adoption. Brodzinsky and Palacios (2005) claimed that adoptees have the most complex task in seeking their self. When they live with their biological family, there are indicators that guide them along the way. They can see fragments of their future reflected in their parents, parts of their personality resonate in their siblings. For the adopted child, these allusions remain open (Brodzinsky & Palacios, 2005).

Noi-Sharav makes a similar claim that self-searching among adoptees is accompanied by the constant sense of sorrow and loss. The sorrow is over parents with whom the adoptee is not acquainted, and if the adoption took place when the adoptee was a young child, then sorrow over the faint memory. Loss is felt over additional aspects related to individuality as a result of adoption, such as ethnicity, whether there are siblings, and the sense of genealogical continuity. These losses create vacant spaces in the senses of self and identity.

But these claims are challenged in light of the fact that the body information which the interviewees succeeded in experiencing is so closely identical to the biological sources revealed only much later on opening the adoption file. It seems that the concept known as "body intelligence" may provide a better explanation for the experiences described previously. Perhaps "body intelligence" is the result of an intense will to familiarize with the biological mother and structure a sense of continuous individuality. When the force of this will overwhelms, "inner body knowledge" surfaces. Unconscious awareness, with the opening of the adoption file, proves its relevance. A further explanation, provided by Waterman (2000), sees primal, uterine and fetal memory as embedded. The memory thus created is a result of the experiences of loss and mourning experienced by the biological mother:

> Children may remember in utero experiences inchoately. We could imagine that adoptive children might pick up their own or their mother's distress in the womb, perhaps even absorbing preverbal communications from their mother on a bodily level….adoptees never get over the loss of the biological mother, her sense of smell or heartbeat, because of the prenatal vessel she provides (pg. 288).[2]

2   Waterman, B. (2001). Mourning the loss builds the bond: Primal communication between foster, adoptive or stepmothers and child.

Waterman's statement indicates that the combined experience of deficiency, mourning and loss accelerate prenatal memory in the biological mother. Perhaps the integration of need, curiosity and questions of body during adolescence constitute a catalyst for making primal body memories accessible. As seen in the interviewees' narratives, the interminable questions relating to body, appearance, genetics and biology encourage compiling a physical narrative. The physical narrative thus compiled is surprisingly identical to the interviewees' revelations on opening their adoption files. It would appear that the deficiency relative to body content and the absence of satisfactory replies create the sense that one of the interviewees termed "living in a black hole". This experience is characterized by what seems like equally interminable waiting to resolve the enigma: to open the adoption file and organize the information that will contribute to consolidating a sequential identity narrative.

2. "Living in a Black Hole": Waiting, Doing Identity, and the Absence of Rebellion in Adolescence

As evident from my interviews of 15 adopted women, their preoccupation with identity during adolescence is complex and replete with content. In the literature exploring adoption and adolescence, researchers claim that adolescence is typified by intensive involvement on the part of the adoptee in establishing the family tree and genealogical roots (Hibbs, 1991 as cited in Deacon,

1997; Siegel, 1989, as cited in ibid). This phenomenon is characteristic of adopted children whose biological background and origins are different from those of the adoptive parents: the phenomenon encompasses blatant physical differences such as skin and hair color, physique, etc. Researchers call the resultant status "genealogical bewilderment"; which in turns leads to the sensations of distress and disquiet. And actually, the findings of the current study indicate that adolescence and deliberations over biological inclusiveness are translated by the adoptees into the feeling of endless waiting – for the biological mother, for splinters of information, to open the adoption file. It is a kind of waiting that receives no resolution but nonetheless shapes a new mechanism characterized by actively "doing identity", initiated by the adopted teens. From the findings of the current study, it is evident that in the framework of "doing identity", the adopted daughters slot every scrap of information into the formulation of identity which is their own, independent product. A further, interesting finding is that within the scope of identity work initiated by the women, there was no room left for the kind of adolescent rebellion so typical of adolescents who are not adopted.

2.1. "And I'm still waiting: waiting for my mother to come, waiting to be 18 years old, waiting to open the adoption file."

> Every adolescent searches for the answer to "Who am I" but for adoptees the answer is much more complex. The adoptee may ask, "Do I fit or belong here, and if not, where do I belong and to whom do I belong?" (Deacon, 1997, pg. 253).

The patches comprising identity, and lapses in understanding identity continuity, are translated into the experience of waiting, an experience appearing frequently in the interviewees' narratives. Throughout, the women described their unceasing efforts at creating a continuum of the life's story despite the blocked doorways to knowledge about their selves. Within such limitations, they experience their attempts as a kind of waiting. One interviewee described her experience as follows:

> For me, age 14 was one of waiting. I just sat, fantasized, and waited for her to arrive. I experienced a very harsh event, and constantly waited for my mother to come and save me. I waited for her. It was like a fantasy. For hours on end, I sat in my room and fantasized about her coming to take me. Only later when I opened the adoption file, I realized, to my sorrow, that she was no longer alive.

Two interviewees claimed that waiting, for them, was tinged with the anticipation of reaching 18 years old and opening the adoption file:

> I counted the days, and one month before I turned 18, I completed the application to the Child Services. I wanted it to work out so that on my 18th birthday, I'd be sitting there receiving details … but in the end, it turned out that the process was a lot longer than that.

The other interviewee's description is similar:

> I think that from 16 years old, I had an imaginary disillusionment chart where every minute and every second were counted until the adoption file could be opened.

In another extraordinary instance, the interviewee described how she and her parents had a terrible fight (adoption occurred in maturity, when the interviewee was transferred from her biological family to her adoptive family, where she did not adapt well). The interviewee described how she was removed from the adoptive home, and physically approached the Child Services:

> Then, it wasn't like it is now, there were no security guards standing there at Child Services, and I simply went there. I was 17, and I sat with them and told them unequivocally, *Bring my mother now*, I was crying and screaming, *Now! I want my mother now!* They said to me, *If you don't leave now, we'll call the police*. And I answered, *So call them, at least when I'm locked up I'll have somewhere to sleep tonight.*

In the end, the biological mother was called to the center that same day and took her daughter home. It seems these actions were directed at immediately bridging the sense of fission in the identity narrative, eventually creating the sense of a self-narrative with internal cohesiveness. It seems, then, that the resolution to the adoptee's identity crisis relies, among other things, on familiarization with the biological roots, and on the adoptee's heritage including race, origin and nationality. Even though the adoptee's original source family, culture and nationality represent only parts of identity, they are vital to creating a complete, independent identity.

2.2. "Doing Identity"

A noteworthy phenomenon surfacing as part of attempts to weave a patchwork of identity derives from the theory presented by one interviewee, who described how she chose her sphere of artistic involvement following a journey in search of biological roots:

> In senior high, I never spoke about being adopted, and I was drawn to certain flavors and foods that we didn't have at home. At this stage, I only knew that my biological mother was Moroccan. I found a friend of Moroccan origins and she became like my sister. There, I found foods and aromas that helped me connect with my mother. It was a kind of curiosity, to locate my mother through taste.

Later in the interview with this woman, she described to me how she was transferred for adoption via guardianship. This meant that her encounter when opening the adoption file was only with the guardians. As a result, tracking her biological mother continues through alternative means, substitute mothers of a kind, and ethnic inclusiveness:

> In university, I really wanted to feel my Moroccan roots. I found the solution through clay. You know, in Morocco there's clay artistry even in constructing houses. I built Moroccan houses, I invested all my money in my studies. I'm so fed up with living in "the black hole" and defining myself as "classical music and fish in tomato sauce". I wanted to do something. To feel Moroccan. I began creating elaborate Moroccan clay utensils. Even when I built my home, I left some money [crying emotionally]. Some money for a trip to Morocco. My origins, you understand? They're my hands and my Moroccan spirit; I take clay and breathe life into it.

A similar story is told by another interviewee:

After opening the adoption file, and deciding only to request details, I wasn't interested in meeting her. When they read the file out to me, I discovered that my mother had lived in a small neighborhood, and apparently went out with a lot of men, and became pregnant from one of them. I was amazed at how similar we were, because during that period I also left my home, rented an apartment in Tel Aviv, and had all kinds of romantic liaisons. Suddenly I could discern the similarity between me and her.

In one instance, the similarity between the biological mother and daughter was based on personality traits:

I didn't want to meet my biological mother, but I did meet my half-brother, who told me that his mother, that is, my biological mother, is a spendthrift. He told me that she goes down to the grocery, to shops, she buys and buys and has things written down on [shop-owners'] IOUs all over the place. And I'm like that too. So since learning about it, that tendency became reinforced in me, and I'm aware of it but I can't do anything about changing it.

Researchers dealing with the emotional states of adoptees in adolescence claim that the possibility of the adoptee achieving "secure identity" proceeds through the integration of at least three factors: openness and containment by the adoptive parents (provision of ongoing knowledge and continuous discussion of the experience of adoption); a supportive and accepting social environment; and disclosure of details concerning biological origins (Hibbs, 1991, as cited in Deacon, 1997; Siegel, 1989, in ibid). Evidently, some components of this equation are absent in the experiences of adoptees in Israel. It should be remembered that Israeli society is pronatalist, viewing birth and biological inclusiveness as important values, such that the adoptee does not always find social support and containment. Furthermore, the fact that the adoptive parents know little about the biological parents leaves the adopted child lacking answers to experiences of clarification and elucidation. The findings of the current study indicate that this deficiency, which may find resolution with the opening of the adoption file, is translated into "doing identity". While collating shards of information, the adoptees weave their own identity narrative. In recent years, identity researchers coined the new term, "doing identity", borrowed from another concept, known as "doing emotion". The term "doing identity" seeks to describe a situation in which individuals consolidate their identity through "identical practices" of various kinds. It seems that efforts at establishing identity and doing identity among the adopted women focus on attempts to create a physical, identical image of the biological mother, especially in light of the absence of clearly defining details. Clearly, the process involves tremendous, varied emotional resources, which as a result creates the surprising and no less interesting process of absence of rebellion during adolescence.

2.3. Absence of rebellion during adolescence

One of the more fascinating phenomena of identity experience in adopted adolescents is the absence of teenage rebellion. This finding surfaced by chance, as a result of the interviewees stressing their definition of themselves as good, devoted daughters to their adoptive parents:

> I never rebelled, and always respected my parents. I knew they did everything for my benefit.

Another interviewee says:

> I never connected with the pranks that my teenage girlfriends
> were into … my working rule was that if you've been given a
> home and a warm supportive environment, then be aware of
> it and appreciate it.

In other instances, interviewees explained that no rebellious
actions were taken because of their adoptive parents' ages:

> When I was 17, my mother was already old and ill. My whole
> adolescence was focused on supporting her and helping her,
> even to the degree of bathing her when she was no longer able to.

One interviewee noted:

> I noticed how my teen friends spoke to their parents. One
> friend had this idea that everything was permissible because
> she was a teenager, and I remember that in my own thoughts,
> I really opposed this approach. If I were to speak to my parents
> the way she spoke to hers, my father would die of a heart
> attack! Her parents were very young, open-minded types.
> With us it just wasn't acceptable that a daughter should talk
> this way, especially to older parents.

I very directly sought to clarify with my interviewees how
they explained the absence of blatant rebelliousness in their
adolescence, and one woman provided an enlightening
explanation:

> During adolescence I was preoccupied with questions of who
> I am and where I am. It didn't start in adolescence. It began
> earlier than that. Maybe individuals who aren't adopted only

begin to deal with these issues in adolescence, which gives rise to confusion and perhaps rebellion. We, the adopted individuals, live with these questions all the time, and it's precisely in adolescence that the questions start to be resolved simply by knowing you're on your way to opening the adoption file.

From the descriptions offered by the interviewees, it is apparent that in adolescence specifically, the adoptees re-adopt their families, but researchers coming across this process never detailed the reasons for its occurrence. The findings of the current study provide at least three reasons for this curious phenomenon. (1) It should be remembered that adoptive parents in Israel tend to be couples who have tried to have children through natural pregnancy, and probably spent several years undergoing fertility treatments. Only on reaching a state of desperation, they consider adoption. As a result, adoptive parents tend to be older when adopting than had they given birth naturally, so that when adoptive daughters reach the age of 18 years, they can find themselves supporting relatively older parents. The interviewees related to their parents' older ages as one of the aspects creating greater consideration of their needs. As such, teenage rebellion is perceived as an inconsiderate action that clashes with the ability for containment and the older parents' needs. (2) From the interviewees' descriptions, the adoptees are clearly aware of the need to acknowledge, and be grateful for, being adopted. This viewpoint translates into actively working through emotions relative to the adoptive parents; manifested conflict and anger do not correspond to the specific family dynamic. (3) The most interesting explanation of all is that teenage rebellion among youth who are not adopted is the outcome of exploring issues of identity which surface relative to devaluing the position of biological parents. But for adoptees, it is precisely adolescence and especially, increasing proximity to the age of 18 that will enable them, for the first time in their lives, to gain some resolution to the open questions of identity that have accompanied the adoptee since the outset of her or his life. Knowing that it will shortly be possible to access the adoption file, which may provide answers to these issues, creates a state of ventilation which possibly voids the need for power struggles and rebellion so typical of this age range.

Adolescence is the first identity-related encounter in which the adopted teen and non-adopted teens are on a par. It is the first time both groups share a realistic common denominator, that of existential issues explored equally by adoptees and their peer group. The current study's findings do indeed show that only in one case, the interviewee rebelled during adolescence. This particular interviewee is differentiated from all the others in that she never knew she was adopted, and only learned of it when she was 17, in the course of an argument with her mother:

> My brother and I were never told that we're adopted. Never. It was a big secret in our home… even on one occasion when [other children] insulted my brother and said to him that our mother is not his real mother, my mother reassured us, *What rubbish, of course you're mine.* Around 16 or 17, I started to get rebellious. I'd talk for hours on the phone, and turn the stereo player up really high. And my mother developed this response where every time it happened, she'd go past with her scissors and cut the cords. One day I was listening to music at its absolute loudest, and she ripped the cable out. I phoned a friend and said, *Can you believe my stupid mother, she cut the*

cable! My mother heard me speaking and then came and cut the phone cable. I got really mad, and said to her, *What are you doing! Now I have no contact with the world.* She laughed but then I swore at her, and said, *You're a whore.*

She was really shocked. Then she said, *Did you call me a whore? Huh? Your mother is a whore, I didn't bring you into this world. You're not from my belly. Whoever gave birth to you is a prostitute.*

And I yelled back, *What? What?* I was stunned by this knowledge, confused, saying irrelevant things. So I said, *What – he's not my father? You're not my mother?* and I ran downstairs to the kiosk and bought four packs of cigarettes. Later Dad came home from work and tried to reconcile, talk to me, explain. I didn't say a thing. Late that night I took a bag, packed all my things and went to my uncle … he [the uncle] said, *Come, my daughter, you can live here meanwhile.* All my relatives came to visit, as though it was a house of mourning … lecturing me on how my parents did everything for me, and that my real parents – well, my father was a pimp, my mother was a prostitute. After two weeks with my uncle, two weeks in which I 'played back' scenes from my life, how it was that everyone knew, and I didn't, trauma, trauma this whole thing. It took two weeks for me to feel I was sure I wanted to go home. When I did go home, my mother continued with the secret and told me that my brother David [pseudonym] must never know. *Never reveal to him that you're adopted, because if he finds out, he'll leave us and there'll be no one to care for us in our old age.*

The description above demonstrates how teenage rebellion, in this case, is the outcome of the first revelation at age 17 of being adopted. However, it seems that the struggle apparent in this narrative is common and familiar to adoptees: the demand that they be appreciative of their adoptive parents who have done everything for them. Understanding that they must show gratitude often puts the brakes on authentic rebelliousness so typical of non-adopted teens.

Rosnati (2005) studied the relationships between Italian adoptive parents and their adopted children, and recorded the interesting finding that during adolescence, communication between parent and adolescent is of utmost importance. In her opinion, communication within the family space is the expression of renewed negotiation between the parent and the adolescent which shapes definitions of separateness between the parents and their children, but also connects with redefining the rules, norms of appropriate behavior, and social skills that the parents nurture in their children. In Rosnati's view, research indicates that adolescents living in the framework of biological families find difficulty in creating the appropriate norms of communication with their parents. She explains this by the fact that communication inherently means closeness, and adolescence is a manifestation of the adolescent's desire for distance and separation from her or his parents. By contrast, it was found that the adopted adolescent displays far more open and continuous channels of communication with parents, firstly because the experience of separateness actually already exists, even unconsciously, and secondly, because the image of the adoptive parent is already magnified in the mind of the adopted child, so that as an adolescent, she or he is manifesting an earlier difficulty, of separating from the adoptive parent (ibid).

Chapter Three

Opening the Adoption File

*Adoptees' Motivation and Loci of Control
When Facing Adoptive Parents and Welfare
Officialdom*

Scientific studies investigating the relationship formed
between the biological mother and her adopted child are
replete with contradictions. Research in the field exposes
the high level of complexity experienced by all parties –
the adopted child, the adoptive parents, and the biological
birther – which exacerbates the difficulty in creating a
comfortable, continuous relationship rather than one
of recurring desertion of the daughter and the desertion
trauma of the biological birther. The following chapter
examines the motives which lead women to open their
adoption file, as well as the types of relationships formed
between the biological birther and the adopted child. The
descriptions offered below will cross-reference with the
literature in the field.

1. Motivated to Open the Adoption File – The Bud of the Biological Relationship, or Attempts to Track the Storehouse of Concealed Information?

All the interviewees participating in the study are women who have chosen to open their adoption files. They were questioned about what motivated their decision. All described their curiosity about the reason for abandonment, as well as the wish to track their biological-genetic inclusiveness. This is what one woman told me:

> Every birthday, I asked myself whether my mother – that is, my biological mother – remembered. I'd ask myself irrational questions, like why she didn't phone me, why she didn't send me a gift, why they aren't ever here, as parents, when I really need them ... what, I'm so terrible?

This kind of emotional flooding is known as STUG – Subsequent Temporary Upsurge of Grief. In *Motherless mothers*, Hope Edelman (2008) wrote that during adolescence, such flooding is experienced when an external reminder comes into play, such as a date, a piece of information, or an important event, arousing new awareness of what has been lost, while bringing to the surface awareness of content which was previously inaccessible (pg. 30). An interviewee describes this experience from her viewpoint:

> On birthdays, which are the worst days of my life, I would ask myself: where is she? Is she crying? Is she thinking about me? Did she light a candle for me? ... You want to know if she remembers at all, if she remembers that on the day you were born, she left you like a grown-up. On every such occasion,

I knew I had to get my answers from her, and this made me curious ... I wanted to talk to her already, to hear what she had to say.

Three interviewees described how they refused to wait until 18. Several days before that longed-for birthday, they commenced their "mission" of opening the adoption file:

For my whole life, I counted the years up to my 18th birthday. It was curiosity: who is this woman? I wanted to see her. So I began from an even earlier age, as I knew it'd take time. At 'a quarter to 18' I sent a letter, and was told that my file would be ordered in. It arrived, and the social worker said, *Your file's here but call me when you are 18*. On my 18th birthday I phoned and insisted on meeting.

Advance preparations encourage the interviewees to open the adoption files before they reach 18. Curiosity is overwhelming, and the possibility of finally receiving that knowledge is translated into pedantic plans over opening the file. Another interviewee had this to say:

Some months before turning 18, I opened the file. I believed that all the mess in my life would be over, the questions of why and how, why I'd been given over for adoption, where my siblings were, my ethnicity – that all those unceasing questions and deliberations would be over at last. I sent an anonymous letter. My adoptive parents really opposed me opening the file, so in my letter to the Child Services I wrote asking that when they reply, to please ask for Dinah [pseudonym]. The purpose was to prevent my parents from catching me out, and if they say that someone called looking for Dinah, then I'd know I should make contact with them. I waited for three

> months, then applied again, and was told that there are
> problems. In the end, I assertively insisted on speaking with
> the coordinator. I was put through, I presented the issue again,
> and within a month a meeting was arranged between us.

This interviewee's narrative indicates that the primary motivation accompanying the newly budding relationship was the desire to find, in the opened adoption file, identity information. Opening the file is an act that translates as resolving identity issues, finding explanations for the abandonment, and clarifying the genetic family tree. Victor Frankl (2000), in *Man's search for meaning*, claimed that the desire to reconcile is the essence of human existence. For Frankl, 'reconcile' meant not only rising above existence, but clearly facing existence. The aspiration to reconcile, according to Frankl, is a manifestation of coping with existential frustration, and where there is no reconciliation, "noogenic anxiety" may develop, the result of deficient knowledge. Situations like these create what he called "psychic stress". Frankl conducted a dialogue with the philosopher Jean Paul Sartre, opposing the latter's views. While Sartre claimed that "man invents himself and he himself shapes his own intrinsic nature", Frankl opined that "we do not invent for ourselves the meaning of our existence *but only discover it*". Frankl's perception is expanded by his views relating to mankind's inability to live in an "existential vacuum" (Frankl, 2001). It therefore seems that the motivation driving the adoptee to open the adoption file and locate those details kept under wraps until that point, reflects the search for existential meaning and reconciliation among the adopted women interviewed for the current study. A further fact supporting Frankl's perception, as surfacing from the interviews, is that women who decided to open their adoption files *much later than 18 years old*, did so after giving birth to a child of their own. Here too, they described their search for meaning, that is, their curiosity over the reasons behind being abandoned, and questions concerning biological-genetics, were central factors in consolidating their decision to open their adoption file. However, these issues were now also bound in seeking meaning relative to their own biological children, driven by their becoming mothers themselves. As such, one interviewee explained:

> I opened my file twice. The first time, I wasn't even allowed to meet her. The second time, around the time when my son was just born, I thought, ok, so there won't be a meeting but at least I'll get some more details. I wanted to examine some fine points more thoroughly, to understand the reason behind my being given up for adoption, what my whole biological heritage is, because now I was responsible for another being in this world.

A similar view was offered by another interviewee:

> After I married and started working [in the sphere of assistance nursing and health] I learned about genetics and genetic illnesses. I was involved with [individuals] with breast cancer, and I had all these new ideas in my head. Eventually I gave birth to my own children, and the business of genetics really bothered me. The desire to finally open my adoption file derived from the desire to understand my own, and my children's, genetics.

The process behind opening the adoption file, as described above by the interviewee, is clearly based on locating information. At this stage, emotional aspects are accompanied by curiosity over the reasons for adoption, but opening the file is chiefly for the purpose of tracking the biological-genetic inclusiveness. This angle appears in the literature delving into adoption:. In Deacon's view:

> The adoptee often wonders what kind of genes are being passed on and feeling about biological parents surface once more. There is often a desire to inform the biological parents that they are grandparents. An active search for one's heritage may often be pursued. The adoptee wants to be able to provide a sense of heritage to his or her own children as well, and cannot do this unless more information is gathered about his or her origins (Deacon, 1997, pg. 254).

Deacon then explains that an additional need surfaces among postnatal adoptees to let their own biological parents know they have become grandparents. I should note that this claim did not surface among the descriptions provided by the interviewees participating in the current study. Deacon expands the discourse about opening the adoption file and examines the stance of adoptive parents whose adopted children decide to find about their biological heritage; this issue was also explored in the current study. Interviewees described how they presented – when they indeed chose to do so – their desire to open their adoption files to their adoptive parents.

2. The Stance of Adoptive Parents and Acceptance of the Decision to Open the Adoption File

Deacon (1997) claimed that the decision to open the adoption file required coping with the adoptive parents. In her view, at this stage the adoptive parents experience repression deriving from their fear of "losing the child" in favor of the biological family. Added to this is the feeling that the adoptive family may expand, and the position of the adoptive parents as non-biological grandparents will not hold. Since the current study seeks to clarify the various spheres of coping experienced by the adopted women, I sought to clarify with them whether they had shared their decision to open the adoption file with their adoptive parents. Of the 15 interviewees participating in the current study, only four indicated that they had shared their intention to open the adoption file with their adoptive parents prior to opening the efile. Nine women claimed that their adoptive parents were not party to the decision: in six instances, the adoptive parents were given a description only after the adoption file had been opened, and in the other three cases, the adoptive parents do not know to this very day that the adoption file has been opened. In all these cases, the women either went to open the file alone or accompanied by their partners. One interviewee describes the situation:

> I knew that if my mother heard I was opening the adoption file, she would feel as though someone had rained on her parade. Suddenly me, her daughter, would be sharing time with another woman... in general, I felt that opening the adoption file was a kind of betrayal to her. She'd show that she's strong, but actually she wouldn't be able to stand it... and that's

exactly what happened. A month after meeting my biological mother, I told her [the adoptive mother], and my [adoptive] father said to me, *Listen, do whatever you want but leave her out of it* … on one hand, I didn't want to censor things any more, didn't want to lie to her … that's also a kind of betrayal.

Another interviewee had this to say:

I functioned as though in the underground, so that no one would know. When they phoned and told me that the file had arrived, I did everything alone. It's just that I was concerned about my [adopted] mother. I was afraid she'd translate it into me deserting her, as though I was ungrateful, my whole life they'd been giving to me, and now I was turning my back on them … to me it was very clear there'd be no kind of connection here, I didn't seek a relationship, I have parents, but I didn't know how they [the adoptive parents] would figure it … I told her only some months later and she cried and asked me how I managed to cope with it all alone.

The emotional investment described by the interviewees is directed at protecting the adoptive parents. The perception that opening the adoption file is a kind of betrayal of the adoptive family relationship is transposed into the complete refrainment of sharing the information:

One thing I knew for sure: that I wouldn't involve my mother in opening [the file]. It was too much for her. For me too. I was afraid of being shamed by what I'd find there, and why should I involve her in such an intimate experience?

Q: What do you mean when you say that you were afraid of being shamed?

A: I figured that someone who gives a child up for adoption is probably not anyone so special, and I didn't want anything of her [the biological mother] to cling to me, I didn't know if she was healthy or ill, if she was normal or not, maybe she looks dreadful ... I was really ashamed. And I was afraid that it would then project on how my parents would relate to me. I felt that it was just too intimate, like taking your underwear off in a room full of people. And to this day, I haven't shared that [information] with them.

From the statements made by the interviewee, above, it appears that the experience of locating and clarifying the information is also accompanied by the feeling that the biological mother's image will somehow project onto the adopted daughter. The idea of such a projection arouses embarrassment, and leads to the desire to avoid sharing the experience of opening the adoption file with the adoptive parents. In other cases, the adopted daughter is aware from a very young age that her parents oppose her opening the adoption file:

In my teens, and especially the closer I got to the age that it was allowed to open the adoption file, my [adoptive] father said, *Listen up and understand this well: I won't acknowledge you anymore if you open the adoption file.*

Q: What explanation did he offer?

A: From his viewpoint, as parents they did everything they could for me, so it's not appropriate now to leave them.

Q: And did you accept that?

A: Yeah ... um, yes. I can't say that I didn't tell him, eventually, some years later. We were in the car and I said to him, *x and y, and if you want, then don't forgive me, but I apologize from the depths of my heart.* And guess what – he said that he had a feeling [I'd checked] and he forgives me. Since then we've never spoken about it.

It seems that no matter whether the message is conveyed unequivocally, or silenced, the interviewees feel uncomfortable in sharing their decision to open the adoption file with their adoptive parents. The journey is a private one, very personal, which may involve shame over who the biological parents are, or shame and feelings of guilt towards the adoptive parents. Interestingly, in the one case of an interviewee who opened the file together with her adoptive parents, she keeps knowledge of continued contact with her biological mother from them.

3. On First Encountering the Adoption File Information: "A Stranger Holds All my Life's Data in Her Hands"

The policy of the Child Services in Israel is such that meeting the biological mother is enabled only after sufficient meetings with a Child Services social worker who prepares the adoptee for the actual encounter. It is a critical stage, in that the social worker assigned to the adoptee holds a central function in dealing with the emotional needs, being attentive to, and beneficially guiding, the adoptee, particularly when taking into account that young women coming to open their adoption file are in the peak of the process of searching and clarifying their identities.

Opening the file is the 'crown jewel' of the identity journey, commenced years earlier, and which will continue to accompany them into their future. They often arrive at the offices of the Child Services charged with the weight of the secret they are keeping from their adoptive families, and the experience of opening the file is simultaneously intimate and alienating. The social worker is the main figure mediating the age disparity, the deliberations and the deficient information, and will fill in, at least at the initial stage, that 'black hole' for the adopted daughter, yet the social worker remains a stranger whom the adopted daughter is also meeting for the first time. The importance of emotional support and attentiveness to the adoptee is obvious. This is the appropriate place to note that public policy would do well to consider budgetary expansion which would allow the Child Services to offer assistive support to adoptees opening their files. The role of Child Services should not end with opening a file and arranging for the adoptee and biological mother to meet, but should support the adoptee further when she marries, gives birth, and so on. All these events occur, for the adopted daughter, as continuing aspects of comparison with abandonment and adoption.

The interviewees participating in the current study described their experiences on opening the adoption file. Two central themes surfaced: the first is the strong need to be viewed as "normal" by the supervising social worker; the second is the overwhelming sense of hierarchy conveyed by the social worker supervising the adoption file's opening, and the adoptee facing that social worker:

On arriving at the Child Services, I was met by a complete stranger. I looked at her and thought: this woman knows more about me than I know about myself. She was very pleasant, and started out by asking me all kinds of things. I felt that she was testing me, how normal I was from a psychological standpoint, how I'd cope with the information. I decided to ask her outright: *Why are you asking me all these questions? Why I came here… what I want to know… Are you checking me?* And she very honestly answered that she was. I appreciated her honesty, and I told her, in response, that I wanted to fill in the missing parts of my identity. She nodded and began to read out sections from my biological mother's documentation … then suddenly at some point, I burst into tears … and she was very sensitive, gave me a tissue … and asked why I'm crying and I couldn't explain it … suddenly, that mother was tangible.

Another interviewee recalled the following:

At the Child Services, I met with some psychologist … she spoke to me, what am I thinking, what do I feel …. I began sensing she was conducting a psychological analysis … I was very afraid that she'd think I wasn't ready and she'd send me back home the way I came. The whole meeting, I was preoccupied with what she might be thinking about me … and the whole time, I kept thinking about how to make her see I was perfectly normal, so that she'd let me hold that file in my hands.

The need to pass the "normalcy test" peaks when meeting the social worker, clearly indicating the inestimable importance and relevance of appropriate emotional support being offered by the authority mediating between the adopted daughters and their adoption files. The descriptions show how the very situation creates a hierarchy between the adopted daughters and the authority, which is perceived as patronizing as it fulfills its mediating role with the adoptee's life information:

> In no other situation in the world does it happen that a complete stranger holds your life in her or his hands and chooses whether or what to let you know … I am furious, angry, boiling at the fact that adoptees aren't able to open their adoption files themselves, as determined by law, and review what's written there.

This interviewee described her feelings of deep frustration at the fact that the information is not given to her direct but rather, is provided via a patronizing, governmental filter. A similar view is held by another interviewee:

> She read it out to me, but I wanted to read for myself. She wouldn't give me the file. And she said, *Whatever you want to know, I'll tell you.* And she's constantly checking that I'm okay, as though I have some kind of problem and she's about to diagnose it … I do understand her position, now, but it drove me nuts that I couldn't take that file and read it myself.

One meeting is described by an interviewee as leaving her with the experience of complete deficiency:

> The social worker told me that in my case, nothing is known about my father. I asked about my mother, and she held the file in her hands and began describing the mother, her occupation, her psychological state, how many children she has …. And I felt it was nothing, just nothing. For any other questions I asked, she had nothing to say … she just said there's no information, no data … I wanted to take that stupid folder and read for myself.

From this interview, it is apparent that opening the adoption file involves a plethora of emotions. The women arrive at the Child Services in order to receive information and complete their identity experience. They presume the adoption file will be placed in their hands, and they will be able to study it freely. The realtime encounter, however, is very different: seated opposite the social worker, they discover that access to the information is obstructed. It is not accessible and free of restraint, but mediated via the social worker. The situation creates frustration, arouses the sense of hierarchy in which one individual, the adoptee, knows nothing of her biological heritage, while the other individual, the social worker, knows all there is to know. The social worker is therefore perceived as the one holding the reins, and the one who will steer it towards the adoptee.

I conveyed this complex experience to Ms. Orna Hirschfeld, Director of Child Services, who is the chief welfare office, and to Ms. Dvorah Shabtai, National Supervisor of Adult Adoptees, in a meeting I held with them at their Jerusalem offices on 24 June 2009. Ms. Hirschfeld made the following remarks:

> The fundamental guideline of the Child Services is to find a balance between the rights of the adoptee, the rights of the adoptive family, and the rights of the biological parents. The rights of the adoptee are the focal point, but preventing irrevocable harm to the biological parents is also of importance. When opening the adoption file, we convey the adoption material in a therapeutic manner. Our work is governed by the ideology that the information is to be conveyed in a therapeutic manner to ensure the rights of both parties.

Here the ethical complexity handled by the Child Services is apparent. On one hand, Child Services employees must ensure the rights of the adoptees, while ensuring no infringement on the rights of the biological birthers. Often these biological mothers have created new lives for themselves, and their spouses and families have no idea of their past, which includes giving a child up for adoption. On the other hand, the burning question is whether every adoptee does not possess an automatic right to trace her or his biological roots, even at the cost of negating the biological birther's refusal to have information divulged. Clearly, this ethical issue also often remains unresolved in the general sense, and the solution is to give consideration to each individual case. Nonetheless, we could say that the interviews clearly show that adoptees are insufficiently aware of the actual process of "opening the adoption file". It would be worthwhile for the relevant government bodies to apprise the adoptees in a preparatory telephone conversation prior to meeting with the social worker about the actual procedure of "opening the adoption file", and at the same time, providing outlines on the realistic course of a meeting with the social worker. Prior updating would save adoptees a great deal of angst and allow them a sense of control during the actual meeting. Heightened sensitivity of this kind would surely go far in serving to dissipate much of the frustration and sense of helplessness accompanying official encounters with welfare representatives.

Chapter Four

"Mommy Dearest" or "You're Just the Biological Birther"

Of the 15 women participating in the current study, only seven actually met their biological mothers. In all seven cases, the meeting included a direct conversation between the two women, and some kind of continuing contact. With regard to the other eight women, two saw their mothers from a distance and initiated indirect contact with other family members, a process which did not lead to any real relationship. One was unable to meet her biological mother: on opening the file, she learned that her mother had already passed away. The remaining five did open their files, but refused to meet with the biological mother. This chapter explores the narratives of women who met their biological mothers and their extended biological families.

1. Meeting the biological mother: an emotional whirlwind

Over a period of several years, Mary Bloch Jones (2000) studied the experiences of 72 biological mothers who gave their children up for adoption. Her book traces the emotional processes involved in giving the child up. The statistics, she claimed, show that from among the half million teens per year giving birth, one in five will place the newborn for adoption. Bloch also noted that pressure on biological mothers to place their children for adoption was a lot stronger in the previous two decades. She explained the altered approach as related to the increasing divorce rate in Western countries, together with altered perceptions on single motherhood. Raising children alone has become an almost normative way of structuring the family unit. Further reducing the tendency to place children for adoption was the significant decrease in the stigma attached to the term "bastard". Bloch Jones noted that several countries removed the status known as bastard from child registration protocols. All these changes helped significantly reduce the number of children annually placed for adoption. Nonetheless, these claims must be reviewed relative to the norms of adoption in Israel.

The Israeli literature emphasizes the traditional nature of local society which values heterosexuality and childbirth within normative couplehood. Of the women interviewed by Bloch Jones (2000), 96% admitted that after placing their child for adoption, they experienced frustration, anger, sorrow and concern for the child's fate. The women described their never-ending wish to trace the child they had given up, and ascertain the child's welfare. By contrast, only 4% of mothers claimed that they continued to function comfortably with their decision to give their child up as a result of having no way to raise the child at that particular time (ibid.)

Israel's closed adoption policy as set by legislation determines that an encounter with the biological mother must be conducted within the offices of the Child Services. The actual procedure takes place as follows: once the adoption file is open and the adoptees express their wish to meet the biological mother, a Child Services employee makes initial contact with the biological mother. If the mother agrees to a meeting, an appropriate time is set. Interviewees described their meetings under the auspices of the Child Services:

They set an appointment for me. The whole night beforehand, I couldn't sleep from sheer nervousness. The morning of the meeting, I drove in my own car and parked near the Child Services. From the parking lot to the actual office was only a short way, which I walked. Suddenly some woman stopped me, she looked the most dreadful thing in the world, her hair was unkempt, she was disheveled, wearing tights.... She touched my arm and showed me a slip of paper and asked: *Do you know where this is?* I looked at her and stopped breathing. I couldn't answer ... eventually I said I don't know. She responded with *OK, OK, never mind, I'll manage.* She turned and went one way, and I went the other. I said to myself, *God help me, if that's my mother, I'll faint!* So I went into the Child Services offices. I sat there in a room with the social worker, and I could hear footsteps outside the door. Suddenly another social worker enters with my mother... and it's her, and she's crying, full of tissues... I looked at her in complete shock, she's weeping her head off and I'm completely apathetic ... stunned ... she'd bought me gifts [details remain confidential] but I wanted nothing, only to flee ... later we were taken to a private room to talk with each other.

A similar experience was described by another interviewee:

I sat in the social worker's office and waited for her ... suddenly I hear voices on the other side of the door, and it's like in a movie, in slow motion, the door opens and you make this close-up from bottom to top... I was glued to my chair, and she entered in high drama, literally screaming, *Here, here's my daughter, my daughter, thank goodness, at last...* and I'm just unable to react at all, I'm completely paralyzed. Then she approaches me and [classified details] and gives me a gift, and goes on, *Thank goodness, thank goodness...* and me – I've nothing [to say].

The emotional outbursts of biological mothers are often met with highly restrained behavior on the part of adoptees who are confused and feel discomfort, then become silent and withdrawn. An interview participant described her experience:

I arrived at the meeting from one direction and she came in from another, and as soon as she sees me she's all over me, with *Where are you? Where've you been? Where haven't I look for you! Everywhere! My whole life I've been looking for you ...* [confidential information]. That's how it was throughout the entire meeting, and eventually we exchanged telephone numbers, but I could hardly talk... My boyfriend was waiting in the car. I said to him, *Let's get out of here, my head's bursting!* That same day I broke out into a rash, my skin was covered in it, itching.

From the information shared here, it is clear that meeting the biological mother is an experience imbued with conflicting emotions, where the mothers release a tremendous outburst that cause the daughters bewilderment and speechlessness. The emotional tension is typified by the mother's embracing behavior, contrasted with the daughter's distancing. It seems that the intimacy which the biological mothers seek to create encounters daughters who